Preschool Favorites

35 Storytimes Kids Love

DIANE BRIGGS

Illustrated by Thomas Briggs

AMERICAN LIBRARY ASSOCIATION

Chicago   2007

Design and composition by ALA Editions in Book Antiqua and Aperto using InDesign for the PC.

Printed on 50-pound white offset, a pH-neutral paper, and bound in 10-point cover stock by Sheridan Books.

The paper used in this publication meets the minimum requirements of American National Standard for Information Sciences—Permanence of Paper for Printed Library Materials, ANSI Z39.48-1992. ∞

Library of Congress Cataloging-in-Publication Data

Briggs, Diane.
    Preschool favorites : 35 storytimes kids love / Diane Briggs ; illustrated by Thomas Briggs.
        p.   cm.
    Includes bibliographical references and index.
    ISBN 0-8389-0938-8 (alk. paper)
    1. Storytelling. 2. Children's stories. 3. Flannel boards. 4. Early childhood education—Activity programs. I. Briggs, Thomas. II. Title.

LB1140.35.S76B747 2007
372.67'7—dc22   3604   2006103159

ISBN-10: 0-8389-0938-8
ISBN-13: 978-0-8389-0938-6

Printed in the United States of America

11   10   09   08   07   5   4   3   2   1

To Kamal and Khadijah,
my favorite twins

CONTENTS

ACKNOWLEDGMENTS

I want to thank all the librarians and storytellers I've known over the years from whom I've learned so much. Specifically in regard to this book, I'd like to thank my friend Lisa Renz of the Utica Public Library in Utica, New York, for helping me to brainstorm ideas for themes. Thank you so much, Lisa, for suggesting I use the following themes: "The Big Bad Wolf," "Going on a Dragon Hunt," "Kangaroo Hop," "Moose on the Loose," "Never Smile at a Crocodile," "Penguin Power," and "Pizza, Pizza, Pizza." The idea for the mud pie snack in the "Marvelous Mud and Beasty Baths" storytime also comes from Lisa. The fingerplays, poems, stories, and songs in this book were either collected from folklore by unknown authors or written by myself unless otherwise indicated. Every effort has been made to find unknown authors, and any copyright omission or credit not given is unintentional. Many thanks go to my editor, Laura Pelehach, for helping me to come up with the format for this book. I'd also like to thank my husband, Scott, for supporting me while I worked on this project. I would not have written this book if not for you. Finally, I'd like to thank my son Tom for doing the wonderful, whimsical illustrations for this book while attending college at the same time. What can I say? You're magnificent!

INTRODUCTION

Preschool storytime is a wonderful world filled with fascinating stories, songs, fingerplays, laughter, and joy. Research on childhood cognitive development plainly shows that storytime programming for young children is arguably the most beneficial service a library can provide. When you present high-quality storytime programs, you will attract crowds to your library. Crowds of happy patrons will cause circulation rates to rise. In addition, pleased patrons will support your library and pass budgets. All in all, it's a winning combination.

After recalling my own successful storytimes and brainstorming with friends and colleagues, I've come up with thirty-five unique storytimes that have been some of the all-time favorites of preschoolers and their families. It is my hope that these programs will create joy and good times at your library.

BOOK SUGGESTIONS

For each of the thirty-five themes in this book I have listed a plethora of mostly newer titles. Although the usual number of books I share in a preschool storytime is three or four, I have deliberately listed more than you can use to allow for personal preference and availability of titles. I've chosen the best-quality titles I could find specifically for reading aloud. Read the books that you love best, and you will have satisfied listeners and successful storytimes.

FINGERPLAYS AND POETRY

Children love fingerplays and delight in doing them over and over again. Don't be afraid to repeat them two or three or four times, especially if your group seems to enjoy a particular fingerplay. Fingerplays work wonderfully as transitions between stories and help release pent-up energy. They are like a glue that holds a storytime together. Most storytime themes in this book include at least two or three fingerplays. When you perform a fingerplay, feel good about perpetuating a wonderful folk tradition.

Present short poems whenever you can throughout a storytime. Use visuals and props to focus attention as you recite or have an adorable puppet recite the poem for you.

THE FLANNELBOARD

Almost every theme in this book features a flannelboard story or poem. It's a wonderful medium that children and adults love. Great storytellers down through time, such as Hans Christian Andersen, have used story figures to help tell stories. When you tell a flannelboard story, know that you are perpetuating a treasured storytelling tradition.

Make story figures using felt, nonfusable interfacing, or Pellon. All can be found in fabric stores. For larger pieces or pieces that need to stick together, use felt. For smaller, more detailed figures such as people or animals, nonfusable interfacing or Pellon is quite easy to use because it is semitransparent until painted or colored. Simply place the fabric on the picture, trace, color, decorate, and cut out. I like to use Sharpies for tracing and high-quality colored pencils or fabric paint to add color to interfacing or Pellon. Flannelboard patterns for storytime themes are found at the end of each section. (You can also download patterns from http://www.ala.org/editions/extras/Briggs09386.) Children and adults alike are sure to be mesmerized by your story figure creations and story-telling. Here are some additional recommendations to consider when creating flannelboard figures.

- Trying to cut felt with dull scissors is no fun. Invest in a pair of good, sharp scissors.
- Use flexible fabric glue such as Aleene's Tacky Glue. Your figures may fall apart if you use other types of glue that are not meant for fabric.
- For eyes, use wiggle eyes, small beads, or sequins, or draw detailed eyes on paper, cut them out, and glue in place.
- Use a Sharpie pen to indicate details or lines. It's a good idea to test your pen on a scrap of the felt or fabric you're using before applying it to the figure you're creating. Have a selection of fine point and thicker point pens available.
- Be as creative as you want and use fun materials such as craft hair, glitter, sequins, feathers, or any other materials that strike your fancy.

ACTING OUT A STORY

After reading a story, sometimes you'll want to give the children a chance to act it out. Dramatic play can add great fun to a storytime. Assign parts to the children and retell the story as they act it out. Some stories that work well are *The Three Billy Goats Gruff* by Janet Stevens, *Big Pumpkin* by Erica Silverman, and *Five Green and Speckled Frogs* by Martin Kelly.

MUSIC

What better way is there to enliven a program than singing a funny song, playing a guitar, or singing along to a great tune on a CD? For each of the thirty-five programs, I have included suggestions for several songs. For your convenience, all the songs are also listed in a discography at the end of the book. In addition to theme music, it's a good idea to use opening and closing songs to help the children transition easily. Here are a few that I have used.

Opening Song: The More We Get Together

(traditional; see discography for tune)

The more we get together, together, together,
The more we get together, the happier we'll be.
'Cause your friends are my friends and my friends are your friends.
The more we get together, the happier we'll be.

Closing Song: Storytime Is Over Now

(tune: London Bridge)

Storytime is over now, over now, over now.
Storytime is over now.
See you next time!

CRAFTS

The crafts that are suggested are easy to make and will add extra fun to your program. The children will proudly show off their work and delight in having something to take home. Most projects require some preparation. I suggest using only washable markers and washable glue sticks when needed.

Storytime Themes

Animal Oddballs

Discover some very odd and always hilarious animals in this storytime. Also featured is the amusing folk song "Down by the Bay," which has been adapted for the flannelboard. Play a funny tune on a CD such as "Be Kind to Your Web-Footed Friends" while the children put together zany animals as they work on the animal oddball craft. Invite the children to bring unusual stuffed animals to the program. Allow them a chance to show and talk about their animal.

ODDBALL READ-ALOUDS

Barrett, Judi. *Animals Should Definitely Not Wear Clothing.* New York: Atheneum, 1970.

Cronin, Doreen. *Click, Clack, Moo: Cows That Type.* New York: Simon and Schuster, 2000.

_____. *Wiggle.* New York: Atheneum, 2005.

Faulkner, Keith. *Funny Farm: A Mix-up Pop-up Book.* New York: Scholastic, 2001.

Feiffer, Jules. *Bark, George.* New York: HarperCollins, 1999.

Lester, Helen. *Hooway for Wodney Wat.* Boston: Houghton Mifflin, 1999.

_____. *A Porcupine Named Fluffy.* Boston: Houghton Mifflin, 1986.

London, Jonathan. *Wiggle Waggle.* San Diego: Harcourt, 1999.

Massie, Diane Redfield. *The Baby Bee Bee Bird.* New York: HarperCollins, 2003.

Monks, Lydia. *The Cat Barked?* New York: Dial, 1999.

Most, Bernard. *The Cow That Went Oink.* San Diego: Harcourt, 1990.

Shannon, David. *Duck on a Bike.* New York: Blue Sky Press, 2002.

Walsh, Melanie. *Do Monkeys Tweet?* Boston: Houghton Mifflin, 1997.

FINGERPLAYS AND POEMS

Five Little Monkeys

(folk rhyme)

Five little monkeys jumping on the bed.   (*Pretend to jump on bed*)
One fell off and bumped his head.   (*Tap forehead with fingers*)
Mama called the doctor and the doctor said (*Pretend to dial phone*)
No more monkeys jumping on the bed!!   (*Shake index finger*)

(*Repeat with 4, 3, 2, and 1. Last line:*
"Put those monkeys straight to bed!")

There Was a Little Turtle

(by Vachel Lindsay)

There was a little turtle,   (*Make a small circle with your hands*)
He lived in a box,   (*Make a box with both hands*)
He swam in a puddle,   (*Wiggle hands*)
He climbed on the rocks.   (*Climb fingers of one hand up over the other*)
He snapped at a mosquito,   (*Clap hands*)
He snapped at a flea,   (*Clap hands*)
He snapped at a minnow,   (*Clap hands*)
He snapped at me.   (*Point to yourself*)
He caught the mosquito,   (*Mimic catching a bug*)
He caught the flea,   (*Same action*)
He caught the minnow,   (*Same action*)
But he didn't catch me!   (*Point to yourself*)

Fuzzy Wuzzy

(folk rhyme)

Fuzzy Wuzzy was a bear.
Fuzzy Wuzzy had no hair.
Then Fuzzy Wuzzy wasn't fuzzy . . . Was he?

FLANNELBOARD SONG

Down by the Bay

(adapted traditional; see discography for tune)

Down by the bay
Where the watermelons grow
Back to my home
I dare not go
For if I do
My mother will say
"Did you ever see a bear
Combing his hair
Down by the bay?"

Down by the bay
Where the watermelons grow
Back to my home
I dare not go
For if I do
My mother will say
"Did you ever see a fly
Wearing a tie
Down by the bay?"

Down by the bay
Where the watermelons grow
Back to my home
I dare not go
For if I do
My mother will say
"Did you ever see a moose
Kissing a goose
Down by the bay?"

Down by the bay
Where the watermelons grow
Back to my home
I dare not go
For if I do
My mother will say
"Did you ever see a llama
Wearing pajamas
Down by the bay?"

Down by the bay
Where the watermelons grow
Back to my home
I dare not go
For if I do
My mother will say
"Did you ever see a snake
Eating a cake
Down by the bay?"

Down by the bay
Where the watermelons grow
Back to my home
I dare not go
For if I do
My mother will say
"Did you ever see an octopus
Dancing with a platypus
Down by the bay?"

Down by the bay
Where the watermelons grow
Back to my home
I dare not go
For if I do
My mother will say
"Did you ever see a whale
With a polka dot tail
Down by the bay?"

Did you ever have a time
When you couldn't make a rhyme?

Directions

Place each animal on the flannelboard on cue according to the song.

MUSIC

The Animal Fair

(traditional; see discography for tune)

I went to the animal fair,
The birds and the beasts were there,
The big baboon by the light of the moon
Was combing his auburn hair.
The monkey bumped the skunk,
And sat on the elephant's trunk;
The elephant sneezed and fell to his knees,
And that was the end of the monk,
The monk, the monk, the monk,
The monk, the monk, the monk.

Additional Music

Funny animal songs can be found on the CD *Rhinoceros Tap: Seriously Silly Songs* by Sandra Boynton. Some of the selections are "Rhinoceros Tap," "Perfect Piggies," and "Turkey Love Song." Also, the CD *Silly Favorites* from Music for Little People has such songs as "Be Kind to Your Web-Footed Friends" and "Snapping Turtle."

CRAFT: ANIMAL ODDBALLS

Cut pictures of animals from old magazines. Next, cut the pictures into parts such as heads, legs, bodies, tails, and so forth. Let the children glue mixed-up animal parts on a sheet of paper to create their own "animal oddballs." You may show them pictures from the book *The Whingdingdilly* by Bill Peet and tell them a shorter version of the story to give them an example of a mixed-up animal. This story is a bit too long for most preschool groups but telling a brief version of the story while you show the pictures may help to introduce the craft. Let parents know that the book may be checked out of the library.

Supplies

Magazine cutouts of animal body parts
Construction paper
Glue sticks

The Apple of My Eye

Display apples of all types in the story area. Hide apples around the room and play a game of apple hide-and-seek. Talk about and tell the names of the different types of apples such as Macintosh, Golden Delicious, Empire, and so on. Cut through the middle of an apple to show the star shape inside. Cut the different types of apples into wedges so the children can taste them. Hand out apples as the children leave the storytime.

APPLE READ-ALOUDS

Bosca, Francesca. *The Apple King.* New York: North-South, 2001.

Gibbons, Gail. *The Seasons of Arnold's Apple Tree.* San Diego: Harcourt, 1984.

Hall, Zoe. *The Apple Pie Tree.* New York: Scholastic, 1996.

Hutchins, Pat. *Ten Red Apples.* New York: Greenwillow, 2000.

Knudsen, Michelle. *Autumn Is for Apples.* New York: Random House, 2001.

Miller, Virginia. *Ten Red Apples.* Cambridge, MA: Candlewick, 2002.

Rockwell, Anne. *Apples and Pumpkins.* New York: Macmillan, 1989.

Rosenberry, Vera. *The Growing Up Tree.* New York: Holiday House, 2003.

Wallace, Nancy Elizabeth. *Apples, Apples, Apples.* Delray Beach, FL: Winslow, 2000.

Wellington, Monica. *Apple Farmer Annie.* New York: Dutton, 2001.

FINGERPLAYS

Two Red Apples

(folk rhyme)

Way up high in a tree,   (*Raise arms up*)
Two red apples smiled at me.   (*Smile*)
So I shook that tree as hard as I could,   (*Pretend to shake tree*)
Down came the apples, mmm, they were good! (*Rub stomach*)

Criss, Cross, Applesauce

(folk rhyme)

Criss, cross, applesauce   (*Draw an X on child's back*)
Big squeeze   (*Hug child*)
Cool breeze   (*Blow on back of child's neck*)
Now you've got the shivers! (*Tickle all over*)

Here Is an Apple

(folk rhyme)

Here is an apple   (*Make circle with thumb and pointer*)
And here is an apple   (*Make circle with other thumb and pointer*)
And a great big apple I see.   (*Make circle with arms*)
Now let's count the apples we've made (*Repeat above actions*)
1–2–3!

FLANNELBOARD SONG

Five Green Apples

(traditional; see discography for tune)

Farmer Brown had five green apples hanging on a tree.   (*Repeat*)
Then he plucked one apple and he ate it hungrily
Leaving four green apples a-hanging on a tree.   (*Repeat with 3, 2, and 1*)
Leaving no green apples a-hanging on a tree.

Directions

Make five apples with the pattern. Before beginning the song set the flannelboard up with all the apples on the tree. Remove the apples from the tree one by one as you sing the song.

MUSIC

Sing or play "Apples and Bananas" from Raffi's CD *One Light One Sun.* The music for "Five Green Apples" flannelboard activity may be found on the CD *Mainly Mother Goose,* from Sharon, Lois, and Bram.

CRAFT: APPLE TREE

To prepare for the craft, cut out tree trunks, treetops, and apple shapes. Let the children glue the pieces onto a construction paper sheet to create their own apple trees. Provide them with markers or crayons so they can add their own details to the scene.

Supplies

Construction paper
Markers
Glue sticks

Bats Are Beautiful

Some bats may be creepy, but mostly they're endearing and cute in the books suggested here. Decorate the room with paper bat garlands or display stuffed toy bats or do both. Several bat poems and fingerplays are featured here, all of which you can also present on the flannelboard. Play the bat songs as the children work on their bat puppet craft.

BEAUTIFUL BAT READ-ALOUDS

Appelt, Kathi. *The Bat Jamboree.* New York: Morrow, 1996.

_____. *Bats around the Clock.* New York: HarperCollins, 2000.

_____. *Bats on Parade.* New York: Morrow, 1999.

Cannon, Janell. *Stellaluna.* San Diego: Harcourt, 1993.

Davies, Nicola. *Bat Loves the Night.* Cambridge, MA: Candlewick, 2001.

Edwards, Pamela Duncan. *Ms. Bitsy Bat's Kindergarten.* New York: Hyperion, 2005.

Mitchard, Jacquelyn. *Baby Bat's Lullaby.* New York: HarperCollins, 2004.

Partridge, Elizabeth. *Moon Glowing.* New York: Dutton, 2002.

Quakenbush, Robert. *Batbaby.* New York: Random House, 1997.

Ungerer, Tomi. *Rufus.* New York: HarperCollins, 1961.

FINGERPLAYS AND POEMS

Five Little Bats
(adapted from folk rhyme)

Five little bats sitting on a gate.   (*Hold up five fingers*)
First one said, "Oh my, it's getting late."   (*Point to each finger in turn*)
Second one said, "There are mosquitoes
   in the air."
Third one said, "Let's eat them up right here."
Fourth one said, "I'm ready for some fun!"
Fifth one said, "Let's flap and run and run."
Then whoo-oo-oo went the wind, and out
   went the light,   (*Clap hands together on "out"*)
And the five little bats flew off in the night.   (*Hook thumbs together and make flapping motion*)

Five Little Bats on a Dark Night
(adapted from folk rhyme)

Five little bats on a dark, dark night.
Five little bats are quite a sight.
Five little bats. Are you keeping score?
One flies away and that leaves four.
Four little bats as happy as can be.
One flies away and that leaves three.
Three little bats swooping to and fro.   (*Swoop hand*)
One flies away and that leaves two.
Two little bats having lots of fun.
One flies away and that leaves one.
One little bat and we're almost done!
He flies away and that leaves none.

(Hold up five fingers. Fly your hand away with a flapping motion and hide it behind your back each time a bat flies away. Bring your hand back with one less finger up each time.)

FLANNELBOARD POEM

Five Furry Bats

Five furry bats were flying by the moon,
"Did you know," said the first,
"Halloween is coming soon?"
"There'll be ghosts!" said the second,
"Floating everywhere!"
"And witches," said the third,
"With long purple hair."
"There'll be goblins," said the fourth,
"And monsters so I'm told,"
"Awesome!" said the fifth,
"Come on, let's go!"
Five furry bats flew off out of sight,
And they will all return on Halloween night.

Directions

Place each bat and other story figures on the flannelboard on cue according to the poem. The preceding fingerplays may also be used with the flannelboard.

MUSIC

Sing or play "The Bats Go Flying" from the CD *Kid's Favorite Songs 2* or try "Fly Little Bats" from the CD *Wee Sing for Halloween*.

CRAFT: BAT PUPPETS

Cover toilet paper tubes with black or brown paper. Or you can simply make tubes with heavy stock paper. Let the children glue on precut wings, feet, face, wiggle eyes, and ears.

Supplies

Paper tubes
Construction paper
Wiggle eyes
Glue sticks

Goblin

Monster

Beach Party

Prepare your story room for some fun in the sun! Display beach toys and shells and dress in beach attire such as sun hat, sunglasses, Hawaiian shirt, shorts, and flip-flops. Invite the children to do the same. Play a recording of ocean sounds for background ambience as you read the stories and do the activities. Go "swimming" around the room as you play the suggested beach songs. Play the song "Octopus's Garden" during the octopus craft activity. Midwinter is a great time to do this storytime. Parents will enjoy the getaway too.

BEACH READ-ALOUDS

Ashman, Linda. *To the Beach!* New York: Harcourt, 2005.

Blackstone, Stella. *Secret Seahorse.* Cambridge, MA: Barefoot Books, 2004.

Freeman, Don. *Corduroy Goes to the Beach.* New York: Penguin, 2006.

Galloway, Ruth. *Clumsy Crab.* Wilton, CT: Tiger Tales, 2005.

Loomis, Christine. *Scuba Bunnies.* New York: Putnam, 2004.

Milbourne, Anna. *On the Seashore.* Tulsa, OK: Usborne Books, 2006.

Munsch, Robert. *The Sand Castle Contest.* New York: Scholastic, 2005.

Ocean Picture Pops: Amazing Photo Pop-ups Like You've Never Seen Before. New York: Priddy Books, 2005.

Peck, Jan. *Way Down Deep in the Deep Blue Sea.* New York: Simon and Schuster, 2004.

Rose, Deborah Lee. *Ocean Babies*. Washington, DC: National Geographic, 2005.

Ziefert, Harriet. *Beach Party*. Maplewood, NJ: Blue Apple, 2005.

FINGERPLAYS

Five Little Fishes

(adapted from folk rhyme)

Five little fishes	(*Hold up five fingers and count down as fish disappear*)
Swimming in the sea	
Teasing Mr. Crocodile	
You can't catch me.	(*Wag one finger*)
Along comes Crocodile	(*Form crocodile jaws with two hands*)
As quiet as can be . . .	
SNAP!	(*Clap hands shut*)
Four little fishes	(*Hold up four fingers*)
Swimming in the sea.	

(Continue until there are no fish left . . . "No little fishes swimming in the sea."
Change the crocodile to a shark, an octopus, or a barracuda if desired.)

My Sea Shells

I found an ocean shell one day,	(*Cup hands*)
Upon the sandy shore.	
I held it right up to my ear	(*Raise hands to ear*)
And heard the ocean roar!	
I found a pretty shell one day,	(*Cup one hand*)
Upon the ocean sand	
With silky colors pink and white	
It felt nice in my hand.	(*Pretend to stroke a shell with hand*)

(Have an assortment of large shells around so the children
may hold them up to their ears and "listen to the sea.")

Catching a Fish

(Mother Goose)

One, Two, Three, Four, Five	(*Count fingers on left hand*)
I caught a little fish alive.	(*Catch fingers on right hand with left hand*)
Why did you let it go?	(*Release fingers quickly*)
Because it bit my fingers so.	(*Shake right hand*)
Which finger did it bite?	
The little finger on the right.	(*Point to little finger on right hand*)

FLANNELBOARD POEM

Ten Little Fishes

(folk rhyme)

Ten little fishes were swimming in a school,
This one said, "Let's swim where it is cool."
This one said, "It's a very warm day."
This one said, "Come on, let's play."
This one said, "I'm as hungry as can be."
This one said, "There's a worm for me."
This one said, "Wait, we'd better look."
This one said, "Yes, it's on a hook."
This one said, "Can't we get it anyway?"
This one said, "Perhaps we may."
This one, so very brave, grabbed a bite and swam away.

Directions

Place each fish on the flannelboard on cue as you recite the poem. On "There's a worm for me" place the worm and hook on the board. Move one fish over to snatch the worm and remove them both from the board, leaving the hook there without the worm.

Note: You may also perform "Five Little Fishes" (see above) as a flannelboard poem. Use the crocodile pattern from the "Never Smile at a Crocodile" storytime on page 145.

MUSIC

Sing or play "Three Little Fishes" from the CD *Bathtime Magic* by Joanie Bartels or "Baby Beluga" from Raffi's CD *Raffi on Broadway*. Other selections are the Beatles' "Octopus's Garden" and Disney's "Under the Sea" from the *Little Mermaid* CD. Play songs while doing different swim strokes as you lead your group in a circle around the room.

CRAFT: PAPER TUBE OCTOPUS

To prepare the craft, cover toilet paper tubes with construction paper. Primary or pastel colors are nice. If you don't want to bother collecting toilet paper tubes, simply use heavy stock paper to create tubes. Let the children glue eight arms to the bottom of the tube in a circular pattern. Use glue sticks to apply glue to the tops of the arms and fold underneath the tube. The arms should splay out around the bottom of the tube. Decorate the tube with wiggle eyes and a funny mouth and nose.

Supplies

Toilet paper tubes or heavy stock paper
Construction paper (for tube and arms)
Glue sticks
Markers
Wiggle eyes

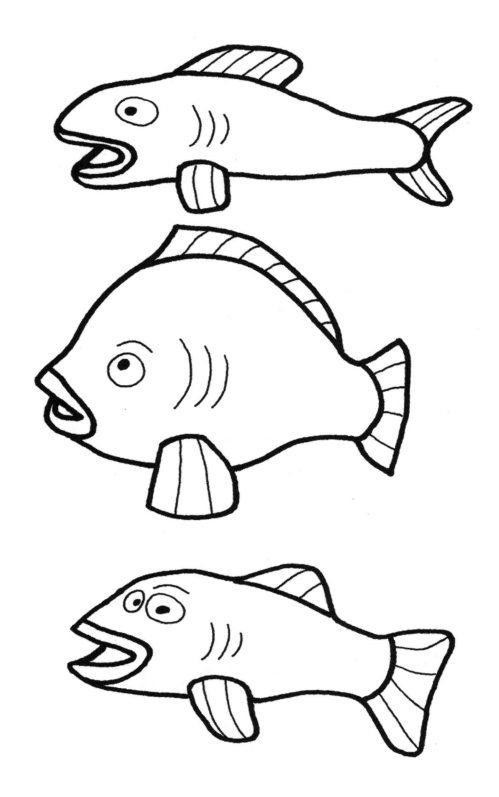

The Big Bad Wolf

"Grandmother, what big teeth you have!" Meet all kinds of wily wolves in these stories. Sometimes wolves can be funny, sometimes crafty and cunning, and sometimes nice. But it's always a good idea to watch out for their tricks. Enjoy the stories and help the kids to act out "The Three Little Pigs." Next, have fun creating a wolf mask. All these activities will make you want to howl at the moon!

WOLF READ-ALOUDS

Fanelli, Sara. *Wolf.* New York: Dial, 1997.

Hartman, Bob. *Grumblebunny.* New York: Putnam, 2003.

Kasza, Keiko. *The Dog Who Cried Wolf.* New York: Putnam, 2005.

_____. *Wolf's Chicken Stew.* New York: Putnam, 1987.

Masurel, Claire. *Big Bad Wolf.* New York: Scholastic, 2002.

McNaughton, Colin. *Oops!* San Diego: Harcourt, 1997.

_____. *Suddenly!* San Diego: Harcourt, 1995.

Meres, Jonathan. *The Big Bad Rumor.* New York: Orchard, 2000.

Moore, Maggie. *The Three Little Pigs.* Minneapolis, MN: Picture Window, 2003.

Perret, Delphine. *The Big Bad Wolf and Me.* New York: Sterling, 2006.

Puttock, Simon. *Big Bad Wolf Is Good.* New York: Sterling, 2002.

Whatley, Bruce. *Wait! No Paint!* New York: HarperCollins, 2001.

FINGERPLAYS AND POEMS

This Little Piggy and the Big Bad Wolf

This little piggy built a straw house,   (*Wiggle finger and on "house"*
                                                          form a roof peak with hands)

This little piggy made a twig home,   (*Wiggle finger and form roof peak*)
This little piggy built a brick house,   (*Wiggle finger and form roof peak*)
And then the first two little piggies went . . .   (*Wiggle first two fingers*)
"Wee wee wee" all the way to the brick home . . .
When the wolf huffed and puffed,   (*Take big breaths*)
And blew their houses down!   (*Blow*)

There Was a Little Pig

(English nursery rhyme)

There was a little pig,
And he built himself a house,
For the Wolf was eating
Every pig he saw, saw, saw.
With a huff and then a puff,
Old Wolf ate him soon enough,
For the silly pig had built his house
With straw, straw, straw.

A second little pig
Built himself a little house,
When he heard the Wolf was
Eating all the pigs, pigs, pigs.
With a huff and then a puff,
Old Wolf ate him soon enough,
For the silly pig had built his house
With twigs, twigs, twigs.

Another little pig
Built himself a little house,
But he never thought of
Using straw or sticks, sticks, sticks,
With a huff and then a puff,
Old Wolf blew, but not enough,
For this pig got wise and built his
      house
With bricks, bricks, bricks.

DRAMATIC PLAY

Help the children act out the story of "The Three Little Pigs." You tell the story (or recite the preceding poem) while the children act it out. Let the children say the classic lines such as "not by the hair of my chinny chin chin!" and "I'll huff and I'll puff and I'll blow your house down!" Choose children to play the parts of the mother pig, the three little pigs, and the wolf. Use a wolf mask (see craft). Repeat this activity if more children want to try it or change the story to include as many little pigs as necessary.

FLANNELBOARD STORY

Wolf's Chicken Stew

Wolf's Chicken Stew by Keiko Kasza is the story of a wolf who tries to fatten up a chicken before putting her in a stew. The ending turns out to be quite different when he meets the chicken's brood of cute little chicks who adore him for bringing so many delicious snacks.

Directions

Obtain a copy of the book and learn the story. Make the house of felt (enlarged) and cut the door so it can be easily opened and closed. Place the chicken behind the door. When the wolf brings the treats to the chicken's house, open the door during their conversation. Pretend to place the treat inside the door, palm it, and place it out of sight. When the chicks appear in the story, place them outside the house near the wolf. Suggestion: Glue all the chicks to a background piece of felt the same color as the flannelboard. It will be much easier to place one piece on the board than numerous small pieces. Display a copy of the book.

MUSIC

The CD *Classic Disney* has the song "Who's Afraid of the Big Bad Wolf?" *Playing Favorites* by Greg and Steve features "The Three Little Pigs Blues."

CRAFT: WOLF MASK

Use the pattern to create a wolf mask. (Enlarge the pattern.) Cut out eyeholes. Color and decorate. Attach a craft stick to the mask so it can be held up.

Supplies

Heavy stock paper
Pom-poms (for nose)
Crayons
Glue sticks
Craft sticks

30

Billy Goat Adventures

"Who's that tripping over *my* bridge!" roared the troll. There are plenty of great books listed here with billy goat heroes. Perform a lap theater puppet play of "The Three Billy Goats Gruff," or use the patterns to create a flannelboard story if you prefer that medium. With plenty of goat songs to choose from and a fun, easy craft, this storytime is chock-full of billy goat fun.

BILLY GOAT READ-ALOUDS

Alakija, Polly. *Catch That Goat!* Cambridge, MA: Barefoot Books, 2002.

Finch, Mary. *The Three Billy Goats Gruff.* Cambridge, MA: Barefoot Books, 2001.

Galdone, Paul. *The Three Billy Goats Gruff.* New York: Clarion, 1973.

Ginsburg, Mirra. *Clay Boy.* New York: Greenwillow, 1997.

Gorbachev, Valeri. *The Big Trip.* New York: Philomel, 2004.

_____. *That's What Friends Are For.* New York: Philomel, 2005.

Gugler, Laurel Dee. *There's a Billy Goat in the Garden.* Cambridge, MA: Barefoot Books, 2003.

Hoberman, Mary Ann. *Bill Grogan's Goat.* Boston: Little, Brown, 2002.

Newton, Jill. *Gordon in Charge.* New York: Bloomsbury, 2003.

Palatini, Margie. *The Three Silly Billies.* New York: Simon and Schuster, 2005.

Sharmat, Mitchell. *Gregory the Terrible Eater.* New York: Simon and Schuster, 1980.

Stevens, Janet. *The Three Billy Goats Gruff.* New York: Harcourt, 1990.

FINGERPLAYS

Troll Man

I am the troll man!	(*Point to self*)
Under the billy goat's bridge!	
I wave my arms! I roll my eyes!	(*Suit actions to words*)
I shake my head! I gnash my teeth!	
I jump up high! I say "Boo!"	
I try to scare those billy goats I do!	
And when I'm through . . . I'm through	
I sit down under my bridge . . . quietly . . .	
very quietly . . . waiting.	(*Sit down*)
For the next billy goat to cross the bridge.	
If they dare!	

Three Little Goats

(tune: "Six Little Ducks")

Three little goats	
That I once knew	(*Hold up three fingers*)
A fat one, a skinny one,	
A funny one too.	(*Wiggle fingers*)
But the one little goat	
With the horns upon his head	(*Use fingers to indicate horns on your head*)
He led the others with	
His trip, trip, trap.	(*Repeat three times; pretend to trot like a goat*)
He led the others with	
His trip, trip, trap . . .	
Down to the river	
They would go	
Trip, trap, trip, trap.	(*Pretend to trot*)
To and fro.	
But the one little goat	(*Hold up one finger*)
With the horns upon his head,	(*Indicate horns with fingers*)
He led the others with	
His trip, trip, trap.	(*Repeat three times; pretend to trot like a goat*)
He led the others with	
His trip, trip, trap . . .	

PUPPET SHOW

"Three Billy Goats Gruff" Stick Puppet Lap Theater Play

Memorize the story of "The Three Billy Goats Gruff" and use the patterns to create stick puppets for use in a lap theater. To create a lap theater, find a box big enough to accommodate a puppet show but still fit on your lap. Cut off the back of the box so you can maneuver your arms inside. Attach a cord to the sides of the box so you can fasten it around your waist. This will help prevent the box from sliding off your lap. Decorate or paint the box attractively or do both. You may even hang small curtains by gluing on dowels as supports. One of the advantages of a lap theater is that the puppets will stay hidden in the box until they make their entrance. Create a set for the story using cardboard. You will need two hills that are connected by a bridge. Glue these to the front of the box or attach with Velcro for easy removal. Make your hills wide enough at the top so there will be room for all the goats. Make slots on the back of the hills to hold the sticks of the puppets in place when you are not holding them. This will make it possible to manipulate the troll and each billy goat with the other goats remaining visible on the hillsides.

MUSIC

Bill Grogan's Goat

(traditional echo song; see discography for tune)

There was a man
   (There was a man)
Now please take note
   (Now please take note)
There was a man
   (There was a man)
Who had a goat
   (Who had a goat)

He loved that goat
   (He loved that goat)
Indeed he did
   (Indeed he did)
He loved that goat
   (He loved that goat)
Just like a kid
   (Just like a kid)

One day that goat
   (One day that goat)
Felt frisk and fine
   (Felt frisk and fine)
Ate three red shirts
   (Ate three red shirts)
Right off the line
   (Right off the line)

The man, he grabbed
   (The man, he grabbed)
Him by the back
   (Him by the back)
And tied him to
   (And tied him to)
A railroad track
   (A railroad track)

Now, when that train
   (Now, when that train)
Hove into sight
   (Hove into sight)
That goat grew pale
   (That goat grew pale)
And green with fright
   (And green with fright)

He heaved a sigh
   (He heaved a sigh)
As if in pain
   (As if in pain)
Coughed up those shirts
   (Coughed up those shirts)
And flagged the train!
   (And flagged the train!)

Additional Music

"Neat Nanny Goat" may be found on the CD *A to Z: The Animals and Me* by Michael Gallina. "The Goat" may be found on the CD *Burl Ives Sings Little White Duck and Other Children's Favorites.* "Bill Grogan's Goat" may be found on the CD *Disney Silly Songs.*

CRAFT: CLOTHESPIN GOAT

Provide each child with a goat body (without legs) made from heavy stock paper. Have the children color their goats on both sides. Glue on wiggle eyes and then add the clothespin legs that will enable the goat to stand. (Clamp two clothespins onto the body where the legs would be.)

Supplies

Goat cutouts (use stick puppet pattern)
Wiggle eyes
Glue sticks
Clothespins with springs
Crayons

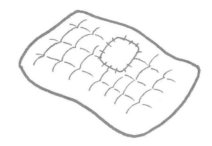

Blanket Stories

G et ready for some warm and fuzzy stories that will make you smile. Invite the children to bring their favorite blankets to the storytime. Introduce the stories with a puppet holding a blanket. Have the puppet describe what it likes about the blanket such as its softness or the way it smells. Then ask each child to tell something about his or her blanket. Next, have everyone snuggle up with his or her blanket and listen to some heartwarming tales.

BLANKET READ-ALOUDS

Gliori, Debi. *Flora's Blanket.* New York: Orchard Books, 2001.

Henkes, Kevin. *Owen.* New York: Greenwillow, 1993.

Hest, Amy. *Baby Duck and the Cozy Blanket.* Cambridge, MA: Candlewick, 2002.

Keller, Holly. *Geraldine's Blanket.* New York: Harper, 1988.

Mallat, Kathy. *Oh, Brother.* New York: Walker, 2003.

Patricelli, Leslie. *Blankie.* Cambridge, MA: Candlewick, 2005.

Ross, Tony. *Happy Blanket.* New York: Farrar, Straus and Giroux, 1990.

Rylant, Cynthia. *Puppy Mudge Loves His Blanket.* New York: Simon and Schuster, 2004.

Stepto, Michele. *Snuggle Piggy and the Magic Blanket.* New York: Dutton, 1987.

Thomas, Eliza. *The Red Blanket.* New York: Scholastic, 2004.

FINGERPLAYS

Fuzzy Wuzzy Caterpillar

(folk rhyme)

Fuzzy Wuzzy Caterpillar
Into a corner will creep   (*Creep fingers*)
He'll spin himself a blanket
And then fall fast asleep   (*Rest head, close eyes*)
Fuzzy Wuzzy Caterpillar
Very soon will rise   (*Wake up*)
And find he has grown beautiful wings
Now he's a butterfly!   (*Hook thumbs together
                                             and do a flapping motion*)

My Blanket

I love my blanket,
It's oh so cuddly
I love to hug it   (*Hug blanket*)
And wrap myself up in it.   (*Wrap it around you*)

I take my blanket with me
Wherever I go,
I really love my blanket   (*Hug blanket*)
Yes I do.

They say when I get big   (*Stand up tall*)
I will outgrow my blanket   (*Raise arm to show how big*)
This may be so
But right now I love my blanket   (*Hug blanket*)
And I'll never let it go.

PUPPET SHOW

Owen

Owen, by Kevin Henkes, is the story of a young mouse who loves his blanket. The problem is he is about to start school. In the end, Owen's mother finds a perfect solution.

To perform this story as a puppet show you will need the help of a few colleagues or volunteers. One of you should read from the book while the others manipulate the puppets and props behind the theater. Or you could record the words, leaving you free to concentrate on the handling of the puppets. It is worthwhile to make the effort to perform this story because it makes a charming puppet show.

MUSIC

Andy Morse sings "My Security Blanket" on his CD *Andy's Funky ABC's.* You'll find the song "Blue-ey the Blue, Blue Blanket" on the CD *Pat the Bunny: Sing with Me,* and the song "Don't Wash My Blanket" can be found on the CD *Peek-A-Boo and Other Songs for Young Children* by Hap Palmer.

CRAFT: PATCHWORK QUILT

Have each child decorate a square of paper with tissue paper, glitter, and interesting shapes using various craft materials. Glue all the squares onto large paper to make an amazing patchwork quilt. Display it in the library.

Supplies

Construction paper
Glue sticks
Colored tissue paper
Glitter
Interesting craft materials

Bunny Hop

Hippity, hoppity, hip, hop, hop! Enjoy this plethora of bunny stories and activities. Invite the children to bring a favorite stuffed bunny. Decorate the room with bunnies. Introduce the stories with a bunny puppet and have it sing a bunny song such as "The Funny Little Bunny" from the CD *Happy Easter Songs*. Enjoy the "Bunny Hop" dance activity and the bunny egg craft, and don't forget Little Bunny Foo Foo!

BUNNY READ-ALOUDS

Bailey, Carolyn Sherwin. *The Little Rabbit Who Wanted Red Wings*. New York: Platt and Monk, 1988.

Baker, Alan. *Brown Rabbit's Day*. New York: Kingfisher, 1995.

Bornstein, Ruth. *Rabbit's Good News*. New York: Clarion, 1995.

Brown, Margaret Wise. *The Runaway Bunny*. New York: HarperCollins, 2005.

Johnson, Paul Brett. *Little Bunny Foo Foo: Told and Sung by the Good Fairy*. New York: Scholastic, 2004.

Krensky, Stephen. *Milo the Really Big Bunny*. New York: Simon and Schuster, 2006.

Lester, Helen. *Listen, Buddy*. Boston: Houghton Mifflin, 1995.

Novak, Matt. *Too Many Bunnies*. Brookfield, CT: Roaring Brook, 2005.

Segal, John. *Carrot Soup*. New York: Margaret K. McElderry, 2006.

Stewart, Amber. *Rabbit Ears*. New York: Bloomsbury, 2006.

Tegen, Katherine Brown. *The Story of the Easter Bunny*. New York: HarperCollins, 2005.

FINGERPLAYS

Here Is a Bunny

(folk rhyme)

Here is a bunny with ears so funny   (*Hold up index and middle fingers for ears*)

And here is his hole in the ground   (*Make a circle with the other hand*)

At the first sound he hears, he
   pricks up his ears   (*Extend two fingers*)

And hops in the hole in the ground   (*Fingers jump into the hole*)

Once I Saw a Bunny

(folk rhyme)

Once I saw a bunny   (*Close fist and extend middle and index fingers*)

And a green, green cabbage head   (*Make fist with other hand*)

I think I'll have some cabbage,

The little bunny said.

So he nibbled and he nibbled   (*Wiggle the two fingers up and down*)

And he pricked up his ears to say   (*Extend fingers straight*)

Now I think it's time

I should be hopping on my way.   (*Hop hand away*)

The Easter Bunny

(folk rhyme)

Easter bunny's ears are floppy,   (*Place hands by ears and flop*)

Easter bunny's feet are hoppy.   (*Hop*)

His fur is soft,   (*Stroke arm*)

And nose is fluffy,   (*Touch nose*)

Tail is short and powder-puffy.   (*Wiggle hands behind back*)

Little Rabbit

(folk rhyme)

I saw a little rabbit go hop, hop, hop.   (*Hop*)
I saw his long ears go flop, flop, flop.   (*Place hands above head and flop*)
I saw his little nose go twink, twink, twink. (*Wiggle nose*)
I said, "Little Rabbit, won't you stay?"   (*Make beckoning motion*)
But he just looked at me and hopped away.   (*Hop*)

FLANNELBOARD RHYME

Little Bunny Foo Foo

(traditional)

Little Bunny Foo Foo,
Hopping through the forest
Scooping up the field mice
And boppin' 'em on the head.

Down came the good fairy and she said,
"Little Bunny Foo Foo,
I don't like your attitude
Scooping up the field mice
And boppin' 'em on the head.
I'll give you three chances,
And if you don't behave
I'll turn you into a goon!"

The next day:
Little Bunny Foo Foo,
Hopping through the forest
Scooping up the field mice
And boppin' 'em on the head.

Down came the good fairy and she said,
"Little Bunny Foo Foo,
I don't like your attitude
Scooping up the field mice
And boppin' 'em on the head.
I'll give you two more chances,
And if you don't behave
I'll turn you into a goon!"

The next day:
Little Bunny Foo Foo,

Hopping through the forest
Scooping up the field mice
And boppin' 'em on the head.

Down came the good fairy and she said,
"Little Bunny Foo Foo,
I don't like your attitude
Scooping up the field mice
And boppin' 'em on the head.
I'll give you one more chance,
And if you don't behave
I'll turn you into a goon!"

The next day:
Little Bunny Foo Foo,
Hopping through the forest
Scooping up the field mice
And boppin' 'em on the head.

Down came the good fairy and she said,
"Little Bunny Foo Foo,
I don't like your attitude
Scooping up the field mice
And boppin' 'em on the head.
I gave you three chances
And you didn't behave.
Now I'm going to turn you into a goon!
POOF!!"

The moral of the story is:
Hare Today, Goon Tomorrow

Directions

Bunny Foo Foo stays on the flannelboard throughout the story until he is replaced by the goon. The good fairy and the field mouse appear and exit on cue.

DANCE ACTIVITY

The Bunny Hop

There are many children's recordings of "The Bunny Hop" such as *All-Time Favorite Dances* from Kimbo Educational and *Dance Along* from Disney. The song lyrics tell you exactly how to do the dance. It's similar to the Hokey Pokey.

How to Do the Bunny Hop

1. Form a line.
2. Have the children hold the waist of the child in front of them.
3. Right foot forward, right foot back.
4. Left foot forward, left foot back.
5. Jump forward, jump back.
6. Jump, jump, jump!

MUSIC

You'll find "The Funny Little Bunny (with the Powder Puff Tail)" on the CD *Happy Easter Songs* from Sony Music. Also featured on this CD are "My Chocolate Rabbit," "Peter Cottontail," and "A Thump, a Twinkle, and a Twitch, or, How to Make a Rabbit."

CRAFT: EASTER EGG BUNNY

Glue craft items onto a plastic Easter egg to create a cute bunny. Glue on wiggle eyes, a pom-pom nose, paper ears, paper whiskers, four paws, and a cotton ball tail. A strip of heavy stock paper taped together to form a ring for a base will allow the bunny egg to stand.

Supplies

Plastic eggs
Construction paper
Wiggle eyes
Cotton balls
Pom-poms
Glue sticks

Goon

Colorful Stories

Y ou'll find all the colors of the rainbow in these tales. Introduce the stories with a colorful puppet that starts a conversation with the children about their favorite colors and asks them to name things that are specific colors. Display toys such as kaleidoscopes or prisms and put up a rainbow picture.

COLORFUL READ-ALOUDS

Beaumont, Karen. *I Ain't Gonna Paint No More.* Orlando: Harcourt, 2005.

Cabrera, Jane. *Cat's Colors.* New York: Dial, 1997.

Dodd, Emma. *Dog's Colorful Day: A Messy Story about Colors and Counting.* New York: Dutton, 2000.

Ehlert, Lois. *Color Farm.* New York: HarperCollins, 1997.

_____. *Color Zoo.* New York: Lippincott, 1989.

Hoban, Tania. *Is It Red? Is It Yellow? Is It Blue? An Adventure in Color.* New York: Greenwillow, 1978.

Martin, Bill. *Brown Bear, Brown Bear, What Do You See?* New York: Holt, 1992.

Peek, Merle. *Mary Wore Her Red Dress.* New York: Clarion, 1985.

Seuss, Dr. *My Many Colored Days.* New York: Knopf, 1996.

Spurr, Elizabeth. *Farm Life.* New York: Holiday House, 2003.

Walsh, Ellen Stoll. *Mouse Paint.* San Diego: Harcourt, 1989.

FINGERPLAYS

Colors

(folk rhyme)

Blue is the sky,	(*Point to the sky*)
Yellow is the sun,	(*Form circle with arms*)
Silver are the moon and twinkling stars,	(*Make twinkling motion with fingers*)
When the day is done,	(*Wiggle fingers in the air*)
Red is the bird,	(*Join thumbs and flap fingers*)
Green is the tree,	(*Raise arms over head like branches*)
Brown are the chocolate cupcakes for you and me!	(*Rub tummy*)

Rainbow Colors

(folk rhyme)

Rainbow purple	(*Form circle with arms overhead*)
Rainbow blue	
Rainbow green	
And yellow too	
Rainbow orange	
Rainbow red	
Rainbow shining overhead.	
Come and count	(*Show picture of rainbow*)
The colors with me	
How many colors	
Can you see? 1-2-3 on down to green	(*Count on fingers*)
4-5-6 colors can be seen.	
Rainbow purple	(*Form circle with arms overhead*)
Rainbow blue	
Rainbow green	
And yellow too	
Rainbow orange	
Rainbow red	
Rainbow shining overhead.	

FLANNELBOARD SONG

Bluebird

(traditional; see discography for tune)

Bluebird, bluebird, through my window.
Bluebird, bluebird, through my window.
Bluebird, bluebird, through my window.
Hey, diddle dum a day-day.

(Repeat with red, yellow, purple, etc.)

Directions

Make a number of birds of different colors and give one to each child. Sing the song and let the children place their birds on the flannelboard when the color of their bird comes up in the song.

GAMES

Bluebird Game

Join hands in a circle. Raise joined hands to form arches. One child, the "bluebird," stands outside the circle. The bluebird weaves in and out of the circle (i.e., through the windows of upraised arms) as you sing the song. On "Hey, diddle dum a day-day," the bluebird taps another child on the shoulder. The child tapped becomes the new bluebird as the first child takes his or her place in the circle. You may assign a color to each child and call out the different colors in turn to go in and out the "windows."

I Spy Game

Example: "I spy with my little eye something pink." Ask the children to raise their hands to answer. Whoever answers correctly gets a turn to spy the next object while the others try to guess.

MUSIC

If Today You Are Wearing Red

(tune: "Wheels on the Bus")

If today you are wearing red
Wearing red
Wearing red
If today you are wearing red
Please stand up.

*(Substitute all the colors you see in the audience,
and then sing the song again, with the following verse:)*

If today you are wearing red
Wearing red
Wearing red
If today you are wearing red
Please sit down.

Additional Music

On the CD *One Light One Sun* by Raffi there is a beautiful song called "De Colores."

CRAFT: COLORFUL BUTTERFLY STICK PUPPETS

To prepare for the craft, cut out butterfly shapes from construction paper. Glue craft sticks to the butterflies. Let the children decorate the butterflies with pieces of colored tissue paper and glitter.

Supplies

Glue sticks
Construction paper
Craft sticks
Pieces of colored tissue paper
Glitter

Cute as a Bug

They're creepy and crawly and sometimes even cute. Introduce the storytime with a cute bug puppet such as a ladybug and sing the song "Ladybug" from the CD *Wee Sing Animals, Animals, Animals.* Show pictures of various bugs and ask the children to name them. Display plastic bugs or stuffed toy bugs or both and let the children play with them at the end of the storytime.

BUG READ-ALOUDS

Brown, Margaret Wise. *I Like Bugs.* New York: Golden Books, 1999.

Carle, Eric. *The Very Lonely Firefly.* New York: Philomel Books, 1995.

Degen, Bruce. *Daddy Is a Doodlebug.* New York: HarperCollins, 2000.

Greenburg, David. *Bugs!* Boston: Little, Brown, 1997.

Kirk, David. *Miss Spider's Wedding.* New York: Scholastic, 1995.

Lillegard, Dee. *The Big Bug Ball.* New York: Putnam, 1999.

O'Malley, Kevin. *Little Buggy Runs Away.* San Diego: Gulliver Books, 2003.

Serwaki. *Doorknob the Rabbit and the Carnival of Bugs.* Berkeley, CA: Tricycle Press, 2005.

Shields, Carol Diggory. *The Bugliest Bug.* Cambridge, MA: Candlewick, 2002.

Walsh, Ellen Stoll. *Dot and Jabber and the Big Bug Mystery.* Orlando: Harcourt, 2003.

Wilson, Karma. *The Frog in the Bog.* New York: Margaret K. McElderry, 2003.

FINGERPLAYS AND POEMS

Here Is the Beehive

(folk rhyme)

Here is the beehive. Where are the bees?	*(Hold up fist)*
Hidden away where nobody sees.	*(Move other hand around fist)*
Watch and you'll see them come out of the hive	*(Bend head close to fist)*
One, two, three, four, five.	*(Hold fingers up one at a time)*
Bzzzzzzzz . . .	*(Wave fingers)*

The Eensy-Weensy Spider

(folk rhyme)

Eensy-weensy spider climbed up the water spout	*(Wiggle fingers upward)*
Down came the rain and washed the spider out	*(Wiggle fingers downward for rain, sweep arms outward)*
Out came the sun and dried up all the rain	*(Circle arms overhead)*
And the eensy-weensy spider went up the spout again	*(Wiggle fingers upward)*

Ladybug! Ladybug!

(Mother Goose)

Ladybug! Ladybug!
Fly away home.
Your house is on fire.
And your children all gone.
All except one,
And that's Ann,
For she has crept under
The frying pan.

My Friendly Caterpillar

(folk rhyme)

My friendly caterpillar	*(Fingers crawl up arm)*
Made its cocoon one day.	*(Close hands together)*
It turned into a butterfly	*(Open hands with thumbs hooked together)*
And quickly flew away.	*(Flap hands)*

FLANNELBOARD RHYMES

Five Little Lady Bugs

Five Little Ladybugs sitting on a flower.
One flew away when it began to shower.
Four little ladybugs crawling on me.
One flew away, and that left three.
Three little ladybugs walking on you.
One flew away, and that left two.
Two little ladybugs resting in the sun.
One flew away and that left one.
One little ladybug flew away home.
She didn't want her children to be all alone.

Directions

Place all the ladybugs on the flower to begin the rhyme. Remove them one by one as you recite the rhyme.

Busy Bugs

Five little busy bugs playing on the floor,
Pussy cat grabbed one, and then there were four.
Four little busy bugs playing on a tree,
One chased a buzzy fly, and then there were three.
Three little busy bugs looked for flowers new,
A turkey gobbler saw them, and then there were two.
Two little busy bugs sitting in the sun,
A hoppy toad spied them, and then there was one.
One little busy bug left all alone,
He flapped his tiny wings and flew on home.

Directions

Place the figures on the flannelboard on cue as you recite the rhyme. Remove the bugs one by one according to the rhyme. Use the tree pattern from the "Apple of My Eye" storytime on page 13.

MUSIC

On the CD *Wee Sing Animals, Animals, Animals* by Pamela Beall, you will find many songs about insects such as "Ants Go Marching," "Baby Bumblebee," "Grasshopper," and "Ladybug."

CRAFT: LADYBUG WITH MOVABLE WINGS

To prepare the craft, cut out ladybug shapes (including a small head) using black construction paper. Cut out ladybug wings using red construction paper. Let the children attach the tops of the wings to the upper back of the ladybug shape using one brad for each wing so the wings are movable. Let the children use markers to add black dots to the wings. Glue on wiggle eyes. Glue on construction paper legs and antennae.

Supplies

Black and red construction paper
Brads
Black markers
Wiggle eyes
Glue sticks

"Busy Bugs"

Elephants You'll Never Forget

Memorable elephants abound in these stories. With flannelboard activities that will mesmerize your audience, great elephant tunes to sing or play, and a fun craft activity, this storytime will be a delight.

UNFORGETTABLE READ-ALOUDS

Archer, Dosh. *Looking After Little Ellie.* New York: Bloomsbury, 2005.

Gorbachev, Valeri. *Big Little Elephant.* Orlando: Harcourt, 2005.

Hanel, Wolfram. *Little Elephant's Song.* New York: North-South, 2000.

Heide, Florence Perry. *That's What Friends Are For.* Cambridge, MA: Candlewick, 2003.

Kasza, Keiko. *The Mightiest.* New York: Putnam, 2001.

McGory, Anik. *Kidogo.* New York: Bloomsbury, 2005.

McKee, David. *Elmer and the Lost Teddy.* New York: Lothrop, Lee, and Shepard, 1999.

Murphy, Jill. *Five Minutes' Peace.* New York: Putnam, 1986.

Salerno, Steven. *Little Trumbo.* New York: Cavendish, 2003.

Smith, Maggie. *Paisley.* New York: Knopf, 2004.

FINGERPLAYS AND POEMS

The Elephant

(folk rhyme)

The elephant goes
Like this and that.　　　　(*Sway back and forth*)
He's terribly big,　　　　(*Stand and stretch arms up*)
And he's terribly fat.　　　　(*Stretch arms out to sides*)
He has no fingers,　　　　(*Wiggle fingers*)
He has no toes,　　　　(*Reach down and touch toes*)
But, goodness gracious,
What a nose!　　　　(*Clasp hands, straighten arms,
and sway them back and forth*)

The Elephant Looks Like a Giant

(folk rhyme)

The elephant looks like a giant.
He is wrinkled and he is strong.
He has two big floppy ears,
And a nose that's oh so long.
He sways back and forth
Through the jungle he goes
With his big floppy ears
And his hose of a nose.

The Elephant Has a Great Big Trunk

(folk rhyme)

The elephant has a great big trunk
That goes swinging to and fro.　　　　(*Clasp hands to make trunk swing*)
And he has teeny, tiny eyes
That show him where to go.　　　　(*Point to eyes*)
His great big ears go flopping　　　　(*Put hands to ears*)
While his great big feet go stomping,
　　stomping, stomping.　　　　(*Stomp feet*)

DRAMATIC PLAY

Retell the story of *Elmer and the Lost Teddy* by David McKee while the children act it out. Choose children to play the parts of the baby elephant, Elmer, Wilber, and the other jungle animals. Add more animals to the story if necessary so everyone gets a chance to play. For props you will need two teddy bears. Hide one teddy somewhere in the room. Let only the child acting out Wilber know where it is. Having the children act out this story is a wonderful way to teach kindness.

FLANNELBOARD STORY

Elephant in a Well

Elephant in a Well by Marie Hall Ets is the story of a young elephant who falls in a well and can't get out. Six animals get together and try to pull him out. Not until a mouse shows up to help does the elephant finally pop out of the well. The story line is quite similar to the classic folktale *The Turnip* in which several people and animals get together to try to pull a huge turnip from the ground.

Directions

Locate a copy of the book and learn the story. When telling the story, start with the lower half of the elephant's body covered by the well so he appears to be stuck. Line the animals up one by one according to the story as they try to pull the elephant from the well. When the elephant is pulled out of the well, remove the well and place the elephant upright on the flannelboard to end the story.

FLANNELBOARD SONG

One Elephant

(see discography for tune)

One elephant went out to play,
Upon a spider's web one day.
He had such enormous fun,
He asked another elephant to come.

Two elephants went out to play . . .
Three elephants went out to play . . .
Four elephants went out to play . . .
Five elephants went out to play.

But, no more elephants came that day!

(*Use the small elephant [make five] and spider web
patterns for the flannelboard.*)

MUSIC

You'll find the song "Elephant Is Sitting in My Bathtub" on the CD *I Love My Shoes* by Eric Ode. "Walk Like an Elephant" may be found on the CD *Songs from JoJo's Circus* by Disney.

CRAFT: ELEPHANT MASK

Cut eyeholes in paper plates or use round pieces of gray, heavy stock paper. Glue on big ears, trunks, and tusks. Fold the trunks in an accordion pattern (before gluing) to make them look wrinkled. Glue a craft stick to the bottom.

Supplies

Paper plates or gray paper
Construction paper
Glue sticks
Craft sticks

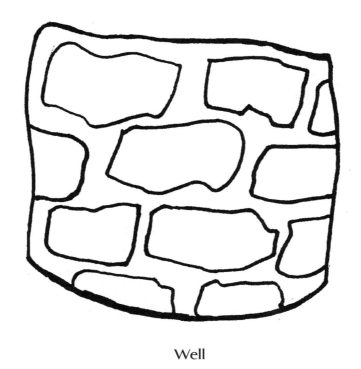

Well

Friends Are Special People

"**M**ay I bring a friend?" "My dear, my dear, any friend of our friend is welcome here." Delight in this celebration of friendship with wonderful stories, fingerplays, friendship tunes, and a cute craft. Introduce the storytime with a talking mouth puppet. Have the puppet sing "The More We Get Together."

FRIENDSHIP READ-ALOUDS

Chichester Clark, Emma. *Will and Squill.* Minneapolis: Carolrhoda, 2006.

Chodos-Irvine, Margaret. *Best Best Friends.* Orlando: Harcourt, 2006.

Dunrea, Oliver. *Gossie and Gertie.* Boston: Houghton Mifflin, 2002.

Edwards, Pamela Duncan. *Gigi and Lulu's Gigantic Fight.* New York: Katherine Tegen Books, 2004.

Elliott, Laura. *Hunter's Best Friend at School.* New York: HarperCollins, 2002.

Jahn-Clough, Lisa. *Alicia's Best Friends.* Boston: Houghton Mifflin, 2003.

Rodman, Mary Ann. *My Best Friend.* New York: Viking, 2005.

Rohmann, Eric. *My Friend Rabbit.* New Milford, CT: Roaring Brook, 2002.

Thompson, Lauren. *Little Quack's New Friend.* New York: Simon and Schuster, 2006.

Wilson, Karma. *Bear's New Friend.* New York: Margaret K. McElderry, 2006.

Woloson, Eliza. *My Friend Isabelle.* Bethesda, MD: Woodbine, 2003.

FINGERPLAYS

Here's a Cup of Tea

(folk rhyme)

Here's a cup, and here's a cup   (*Make circles with thumbs and index fingers on each hand and extend arms*)

And here's a pot of tea.   (*Make fist with one hand, extend thumb for spout*)

Pour a cup, and pour a cup   (*Tip fist to pour*)

And have a drink with me.   (*Make drinking motions*)

Look at the Apple I Have Found

(folk rhyme)

Look at the apple I have found   (*Circle hands*)

So round and rosy on the ground.

We will wash it and cut it in two   (*Perform actions*)

Half for me and half for you.   (*Hold out both hands*)

Two Little Friends

(folk rhyme)

Two little friends are better than one,   (*Hold up two fingers on right hand, one on left*)

And three are better than two   (*Three on left, and two on right*)

And four are much better still.   (*Four on right hand*)

Just think!

What four little friends can do!

FLANNELBOARD STORY

May I Bring a Friend?

May I Bring a Friend? by Beatrice Schenk de Regniers, 1965 Caldecott Medal winner, is the story of a little boy who brings his animal friends to visit the King and Queen.

Directions

Obtain a copy of the book and learn the story. The text is written in rhyme so you may want to print out a "cheat sheet" to refer to while presenting the story. Attach it to the side of the easel behind your flannelboard or use some other arrangement so you can refer to the sheet without it being seen. Use the giraffe, lion, and hippo patterns from the "Moonkey" flannelboard story on pages 126–128.

Use the elephant pattern from the "Elephant in a Well" story on page 66. Place each animal on the flannelboard and remove the animals in turn according to the story. At the end of the story, place all the characters on the board. Display the book.

MUSIC

The More We Get Together

(traditional)

The more we get together, together, together,
The more we get together, the happier we'll be.
'Cause your friends are my friends and my friends are your friends.
The more we get together, the happier we'll be.

Additional Music

"We're Going to Be Friends" may be found on the CD *Curious George and Friends: Sing-a-longs and Lullabies,* and "Friends Are Everywhere" may be found on the CD *Monkey's Uncle* by Uncle Brothers.

CRAFT: POM-POM FRIENDS

Glue two large pom-poms (two friends) to an index card. Glue on little felt arms and legs, wiggle eyes, noses, smiles, and so forth. Parental help may be needed for this craft.

Supplies

Pom-poms   Felt pieces
Glue   Wiggle eyes

Gingerbread Stories

R un, run, run as fast as you can! You can't catch me. . . ." Enjoy the warm, spicy sweetness of these stories. Have fun performing a stick puppet play, and show the kids how to create a cute little gingerbread house to take home, display, and, eventually, eat!

GINGERBREAD READ-ALOUDS

Aylesworth, Jim. *The Gingerbread Man.* New York: Scholastic, 1998.

Bratun, Katy. *Gingerbread Mouse.* New York: HarperCollins, 2003.

Brett, Jan. *Gingerbread Baby.* New York: Putnam, 1999.

Cousins, Lucy. *Maisy Makes Gingerbread.* Cambridge, MA: Candlewick, 1999.

Ernst, Lisa Campbell. *The Gingerbread Girl.* New York: Dutton, 2006.

Galdone, Paul. *The Gingerbread Boy.* New York: Clarion, 1975.

Hillert, Margaret. *The Little Cookie.* Cleveland: Modern Curriculum Press, 1981.

Parker, Toni Trent. *Snowflake Kisses and Gingerbread Smiles.* New York: Scholastic, 2002.

Squires, Janet. *The Gingerbread Cowboy.* New York: Laura Geringer, 2006.

FINGERPLAYS

Gingerbread People

Five little gingerbread boys/girls all in a row,   (*Hold up five fingers*)
Each with frosting and a big red bow.
"You can't catch me!" one did say   (*Wiggle one finger*)
And that little gingerbread boy/girl ran away!   (*Fold one finger down*)
Four little . . .
Three little . . .
Two little . . .
One little gingerbread boy/girl ready to go says:
"Run, run as fast as you can!
You can't catch me! I'm the gingerbread man!
Bye, bye!"

(Idea: Choose five children to act out this rhyme as you recite it.
Repeat it until all children have had a chance. This rhyme may also
be used with finger puppets or the flannelboard.)

Gingerbread
(folk rhyme)

Stir a bowl of gingerbread   (*Make stirring motion*)
Smooth and spicy brown.
Roll it with a rolling pin   (*Pretend to roll dough*)
Up and up and down.
With a cookie cutter   (*Pretend to cut cookies with cutter*)
Make some little men,
Put them in the oven   (*Put tray in the oven*)
Until half past ten.

PUPPET SHOW

"The Gingerbread Boy" Stick Puppet Lap Theater Play

Memorize the story of "The Gingerbread Boy" and use the patterns to create
stick puppets for use in a lap theater. (To create a lap theater, see the directions
on page 36 in the "Billy Goat Adventures" storytime. The stick puppet patterns
are located at the end of this section.)

MUSIC

You'll find "Gingerbread Man" on the Sesame Street CD *"C" Is for Cookie: Cookie's Favorite Songs.* Joe Scruggs also sings "The Gingerbread Man" on his CD *Bahamas Pajamas.* In addition, Teresa Brewer sings "The Gingerbread House" on her CD *Down the Holiday Trail.*

CRAFT: GINGERBREAD HOUSE

Use graham crackers and ready-to-spread frosting to create a miniature gingerbread house. An inner structure of a washed, pint-size milk carton may help with the construction. Add gumdrops, Necco wafers for roofing, mini-cookies, peppermints, licorice, M&Ms, or whatever else you like.

Supplies

Graham crackers
Frosting
Milk cartons (washed)
Various candies

Going on a Dragon Hunt

"It's hard to stop Muggles from noticing us if we're keeping dragons in the back garden" (Ron Weasley). Enjoy these fascinating stories about our fire breathing friends. Have fun performing the "repeat after me" action chant, "We're Going on a Dragon Hunt," which is adapted from the traditional chant, "We're Going on a Bear Hunt." "The Foolish Dragon" flannelboard story is based on a folktale from China.

DRAGON READ-ALOUDS

Baumgart, Klaus. *Anna and the Little Green Dragon.* New York: Hyperion, 1992.

Berkeley, Jon. *Chopsticks.* New York: Random House, 2002.

Bertrand, Lynne. *Dragon Naps.* New York: Viking, 1996.

Hunter, Jana Novotny. *Little Ones Do!* New York: Dutton, 2001.

Kent, Jack. *There's No Such Thing as a Dragon.* New York: Golden Press/ Western, 1975.

Mayhew, James. *Who Wants a Dragon?* New York: Orchard Books, 2004.

Meddaugh, Susan. *Harry on the Rocks.* Boston: Houghton Mifflin, 2003.

Roberts, Bethany. *Gramps and the Fire Dragon.* New York: Clarion, 1997.

Robertson, M. P. *The Egg.* New York: Puffin, 2000.

Tanis, Joel. *The Dragon Pack Snack Attack.* New York: Four Winds, 1993.

Thayer, Jane. *The Popcorn Dragon*. New York: Morrow, 1989.

Thomas, Shelley Moore. *Good Night, Good Knight*. (Series) New York: Dutton, 2000.

ACTION CHANT

We're Going on a Dragon Hunt Action Chant

(adapted from "We're Going on a Bear Hunt")

(*Instruct the children to repeat each phrase.*)

We're going on a dragon hunt.	(*Slap thighs alternately in rhythm*)
We're gonna catch a big one.	
We're not scared.	
Oh, oh.	
What's this?	
Tall grass.	
We can't go over it.	
We can't go under it.	
We've got to go through it.	
Swishy, swashy, swishy, swashy.	(*Make arm motions as if you're making your way through tall grass*)
We're going on a dragon hunt.	(*Slap thighs alternately in rhythm*)
We're gonna catch a big one.	
We're not scared.	
Oh, oh.	
What's this?	
Mud.	
Thick gooey mud.	
We can't go over it.	
We can't go under it.	
We've got to go through it.	
Squishy, squelchy, squishy, squelchy.	(*Pretend to walk through thick mud*)
We're going on a dragon hunt.	(*Slap thighs alternately in rhythm*)
We're gonna catch a big one.	
We're not scared.	
Oh, oh.	
What's this?	
A river.	
A *wide* river.	

We can't go over it.
We can't go under it.
We've got to swim across it.
Splishy, splashy, splishy, splashy.   (*Do swimming motions*)

We're going on a dragon hunt.   (*Slap thighs alternately in rhythm*)
We're gonna catch a big one.
We're not scared.
Oh, oh.
What's this?
A tree.
A tall tree.
We can't go over it.
We can't go under it.
We've got to climb up it.
Up, up, up, up, up.   (*Do climbing motions*)

We're going on a dragon hunt.   (*Slap thighs alternately in rhythm*)
We're gonna catch a big one.
We're not scared.
Oh, oh.
What's this?
A cave.
A deep, dark cave.
We can't go over it.
We can't go under it.
We've got to go in it.
Oh, oh.
It's really dark in here.
I can't see.
What's this?
It feels rough.
It feels like scales!
And I feel some long, sharp teeth and hot, hot breath!
Ahhhhhhhhh!!!!!!
It's a dragon!!!
Run!   (*Alternately slap thighs much faster*)
Climb up and down the tree! . . . up,
    up, up . . . down, down, down.
Swim across the river! Do the dog
    paddle fast!!! . . . splishy, splashy, splishy, splashy.
Run through the mud . . . squishy, squelchy, squishy, squelchy.
Run through the grass . . . swishy, swashy, swishy, swashy.
Run into your house.
Slam the door . . . bang!
And lock it . . . click.

Woooo! We're safe.
I'm not scared.
Are you?
Not me!!!

FLANNELBOARD STORY

The Foolish Dragon

(adapted from a Chinese tale)

Long ago and far away in the country of China there lived a dragon and his beautiful dragon wife. One day Mrs. Dragon got a craving for something to eat and told Mr. Dragon she was hungry.

"Dear, would you get me a special something to eat?" she said.

"Yes, my love, anything your heart desires," replied the dragon.

"Well, I want a monkey's heart to eat."

"My dear, monkeys live up in trees in the high mountains! It will be quite difficult to get one of their hearts. I don't know if it's possible."

"Well, nothing else will satisfy me. I must have a monkey's heart or I will become very irritable. If I start breathing heavy it's possible I could burn the place down. I need a monkey's heart and I need it now. There is just no getting around it."

Without delay, but quite unsure of himself, the dragon set out to the mountains. When he spied a monkey on top of a tree, he shouted: "Hey, there, young fellow, aren't you afraid of falling?"

"No, not particularly," the monkey answered.

"Well, another thing I was wondering, why do you eat the dried-up fruit from that tree when across the sea on yonder island there is an abundance of ripe, juicy fruit?"

"How would I get over there?"

"Get on my back. I'll give you a ride."

Then the dragon with the little monkey on his back set out to sea for the island. Suddenly, without warning, the dragon took a dive.

"What are you doing? I'm going to drown!" spluttered the monkey with salt water in his mouth, nose, and eyes.

"I'm sorry little fellow, but Mrs. Dragon wants to eat your heart and I must do what I have to do."

The monkey had to think fast to come up with a way to save himself and said, "Mr. Dragon, why didn't you tell me before? I will gladly give my heart to Mrs. Dragon if she wants it, but I left it up in the tree on the shore. You must take me back and I will get it."

The dragon returned to the shore and the monkey scampered back up the tree. After waiting for a time the dragon realized the monkey was taking quite a while to come down. So he said, "Hurry up, little fellow. I'm waiting."

All the monkey could think was: "This is one foolish dragon."

Soon the dragon tired of waiting and went away. As for the clever little monkey, he kept his heart for ever more. The End.

Directions

Use the palm tree pattern from the "Moonkey" flannelboard story on page 129. For the opening scene, place the two dragons on the flannelboard. For the second scene, place the tree on one side of the flannelboard and a long piece of blue felt to represent the water on the other side. Put the monkey up in the tree. Put him on the dragon's back when they go in the "water." Place him back in the tree at the end of the story.

MUSIC

Sing or play a recording of "Puff the Magic Dragon." It's on Peter, Paul, and Mary's album *Peter, Paul, and Mommy.* On Tom Knight's CD *The Library Boogie* you'll also find the tune "Sally and the Dragon."

CRAFT: DRAGON PAPER SCULPTURE

Use heavy stock paper and tape to create tubes. Make them as large as you like. The tube is the dragon's body. Cut a V-shaped hole in the tube where the mouth should be. Let the children glue on little paper teeth and a paper flame. In addition let them glue on simple construction paper cutouts (that you prepare ahead of time) for the arms, legs, tail, wings, and back fins. Provide the children with sequins, wiggle eyes, feathers, or other craft materials so they can create their own unique dragons.

Supplies

Heavy stock paper
Construction paper
Glue sticks
Sequins
Wiggle eyes
Feathers for wings
Markers

Kangaroo Hop

Boing! Boing! Boing! These stories have lots of bounce! Decorate the story area with pictures of kangaroos and kangaroo stuffed toys if you have them. Introduce the stories with a kangaroo puppet and discuss kangaroos with the children. Play kangaroo music such as "Tie Me Kangaroo Down Sport," sung by the Wiggles musical group, as you hop about the room. As for the craft, not many paper bag puppets have pouches . . . but this one does.

KANGAROO READ-ALOUDS

Bruel, Nick. *Boing.* Brookfield, CT: Roaring Brook, 2004.

Chichester Clark, Emma. *I Love You, Blue Kangaroo!* New York: Scholastic, 2001.

Davis, Katie. *Who Hops?* San Diego: Harcourt, 1998.

Dodds, Siobhan. *Grumble! Rumble!* New York: Dorling Kindersley, 2000.

Edwards, Pamela Duncan. *McGillycuddy Could!* New York: Katherine Tegen, 2005.

Genechten, Guido van. *Kangaroo Christine.* Wilton, CT: Tiger Tales, 2006.

Kent, Jack. *Joey Runs Away.* Englewood Cliffs, NJ: Prentice-Hall, 1985.

Levitin, Sonia. *When Kangaroo Goes to School.* Flagstaff, AZ: Rising Moon, 2001.

Payne, Emmy. *Katy No-Pocket.* Boston: Houghton Mifflin, 1972.

Vaughan, Marcia. *Snap!* New York: Scholastic, 1996.

FINGERPLAYS AND POEMS

What about the Kangaroo?

Crabs walk sideways,   (*Move sideways and make hands into pincers*)
What a funny way to go.
An elephant walks forwards   (*Move forward slowly with arms like a trunk*)
Very, very slow.
Penguins waddle, waddle,   (*Waddle with arms straight at sides*)
And that is funny too,
But what about the hopping
Of a great, big kangaroo.   (*Hop around*)

Hopping Kangaroo

(folk rhyme)

The hopping kangaroo is very funny,
She leaps and jumps and hops like a bunny,   (*Hop up and down*)
And on her stomach is a pocket so wide,   (*Place hand on stomach like a pocket*)
Her baby can jump in and go for a ride!

Jumping Kangaroo

(*Suit actions to words*)

Jump! Jump! Jump!   Jump! Jump! Jump!
Kangaroo Jack!   Up hill and down!
Jump! Jump! Jump!   Jump! Jump! Jump!
Let's give it a crack!   All over the town!

Do Like the Animals Do

(*Suit actions to words*)

Jump, jump, jump, like a frog
Run, run, run, like a deer
Fly, fly, fly, like a birdie too
And don't forget to hop like a kangaroo!

FLANNELBOARD POEM

Little Lost Joey

There was a little, lost joey
Whose name was Sonny Jim.
His mommy seemed to be missing.
Oh what a fix he was in!

He asked a duck if she'd seen her
As she was waddling down the road.
The duck looked around in the area
And said, "I can't find her, dear, no."

He asked a funny platypus
If his mommy *he* could find.
But the platypus shook his duck-billed head
And said, "I just don't have the time."

Next he asked a koala
With a sweet, little teddy bear face
If he had seen his mommy
And the koala said, "No, not a trace."

Next came a chubby old wombat
And the joey asked her too
And when she couldn't help him
He just didn't know what to do.

It was then that a kookaburra
Flying high and as free as can be
Said, "Sonny Jim, dry up your tear drops.
She's napping right under that tree."

Sonny Jim jumped for joy
And ran to his mommy with glee.
He hopped in her pouch
Like a fuzzy old couch
And they jumped away happily.

Directions

Place the joey on the flannelboard and add each character on cue according to the poem. On "ran to his mommy with glee," place the mother kangaroo on the board and put the joey in her pouch. Glue on the pouch so it is loose and open at the top and easy to insert the joey into.

MUSIC

You'll find "Tie Me Kangaroo Down Sport" on the CD *Wiggly, Wiggly World* by the Wiggles (musical group). The song "Kicking Kangaroo" may be found on *A to Z: The Animals and Me* from Kimbo Educational, and "The Duck and the Kangaroo" is on the *Wee Sing Animals, Animals, Animals* CD.

CRAFT: KANGAROO PAPER BAG PUPPET WITH JOEY

Glue the pattern pieces from page 88 (enlarged) onto a paper bag. Glue on the pouch, leaving the top open, and put the joey inside.

Supplies

Paper bags   Crayons
Paper   Glue sticks

Kissable Frogs

"Ugh! It's my boyfriend, the frog, at the door," whined the princess. Ribbit! Get ready for some froggy fun. Display stuffed frogs and frog realia in the story room. Introduce the stories with a frog puppet and have it sing "A-Goong Went the Little Green Frog." The kids will thoroughly enjoy the "Wide-Mouthed Frog" puppet play, and the durable pet rock frog craft will be a keepsake for a long time.

FROG READ-ALOUDS

Ada, Alma Flor. *Friend Frog.* San Diego: Harcourt, 2000.

Asch, Frank. *Baby Bird's First Nest.* San Diego: Harcourt, 1999.

Asher, Sandy. *Too Many Frogs.* New York: Philomel, 2005.

Faulkner, Keith. *The Wide-Mouthed Frog: A Pop-up Book.* New York: Dial, 1996.

Kalan, Robert. *Jump, Frog, Jump!* New York: Greenwillow, 1981.

Kelly, Martin. *Five Green and Speckled Frogs.* New York: Handprint, 2000.

London, Jonathan. *Froggy's First Kiss.* New York: Viking, 1998.

Mann, Pamela. *The Frog Princess.* Milwaukee: Gareth Stevens, 1995.

Sweeney, Jacqueline. *Once upon a Lily Pad.* San Francisco: Chronicle Books, 1995.

Velthuijs, Max. *Frog in Love.* New York: Farrar, Straus and Giroux, 1989.

FINGERPLAYS AND POEMS

Five Little Tree Frogs

Five little tree frogs, up in a tree,   (*Hold up five fingers*)
Teasing Mr. Alligator: "You can't
    catch me!"   (*Wag index finger*)
Along comes alligator quiet as
    can be.   (*Palms together . . . make wavy motion*)
And, SNAP!   (*Snap palms together*)
Four little tree frogs, up in a tree,

(*Repeat with 4, 3, 2, and 1*)
(*Idea: Create frog finger puppets using the pattern. While performing the
rhyme snap the frogs off your fingers with an alligator puppet.
The finger puppet pattern is found at the end of this section.*)

I'm a Little Frog

(folk rhyme)

I'm a little frog,
Hopping on a log.   (*Hop finger on palm of hand*)
Listen to my song.   (*Make frog sounds*)
I sleep all winter long.   (*Rest head on hands*)
I wake up and peek out,
And then I jump all about.   (*Jump around*)
I catch flies,   (*Grabbing motion*)
I wink my eyes,   (*Wink eyes*)
I hop and hop,   (*Do some hopping*)
And then I stop.

This Little Froggy

(folk rhyme)

This little froggy took a big leap,
This little froggy took a small,
This little froggy leaped sideways,
And this little froggy not at all,
And this little froggy went,
hippity, hippity, hippity hop, all the way home.

DRAMATIC PLAY

Let the children act out the story/song *Five Green and Speckled Frogs,* by Martin Kelly. You recite or sing the words. Have the children make the frog sounds, pretend to catch insects, and jump off an imaginary log into an imaginary pond. So that everyone gets a chance to play, change the song to include as many frogs as you like.

PUPPET SHOW

The Wide-Mouthed Frog

(adapted from the folk tale)

Puppets needed: frog with talking mouth, bee, owl, duck, rabbit, and crocodile

(A bumble bee puppet appears and flies around. The frog appears and catches it in his mouth and then spits it out.)

Frog: Owww!! That bee stung me! I'm sick of eating bugs, the creepy crawlers. I'm a great big wide-mouthed frog and I deserve something better!

(Frog sings to the tune of "Wheels on the Bus.")

I am a great big wide-mouthed frog, wide-mouthed frog, wide-mouthed frog. I am a great big wide-mouthed frog and I'm adorable.

(Owl enters.)

Hello, Friend Owl. By the way, what do you eat? I'm tired of eating bugs and I need some new menu ideas.

Owl: I'd be glad to help. My favorite food is a nice, juicy mouse. I swallow them whole. Yum! Yum!

Frog: Well, thanks, Owl, but I don't know if I will like mice. Too furry.

Owl: Suit yourself then, bye.

(Owl exits.)

Frog: I am a great big wide-mouthed frog, wide-mouthed frog, wide-mouthed frog. I am a great big wide-mouthed frog and I'm adorable.

(Duck enters.)

Why, hello, Friend Duck. How are you today? By the way, what do you eat?

Duck: Well, I simply love bread crumbs, especially if they're thrown at me.

Frog: Sounds interesting but I think I need something a little more delicious.

Duck: Suit yourself then, bye.

(Duck exits.)

Frog: I am a great big wide-mouthed frog, wide-mouthed frog, wide-mouthed frog. I am a great big wide-mouthed frog and I'm adorable.

	(*Rabbit enters.*)
	Hello, Friend Rabbit. How's it going? By the way, would you mind giving me some ideas for delicious foods to eat?
Rabbit:	Sure, Frog. Well, I like carrots and lettuce. They're delightful.
Frog:	Interesting . . . but I think I would like something meatier.
Rabbit:	Suit yourself then, bye.
	(*Rabbit exits.*)
Frog:	I am a great big wide-mouthed frog, wide-mouthed frog, wide-mouthed frog. I am a great big wide-mouthed frog and I'm adorable.
	(*Crocodile enters.*)
	Why, hi there, Mr. Crocodile. By the way, what's your favorite food?
Crocodile:	Well, my favorite food just happens to be WIDE-MOUTHED FROGS!
Frog:	I am a little, tiny small-mouthed frog, small-mouthed frog, small-mouthed frog. I am a little, tiny small-mouthed frog and I taste really bad.
	(*Frog quickly exits to get away from Crocodile.*)

Directions

This play may be performed a number of ways. It may be performed without a puppet stage in a storytelling style or performed with a full-size puppet stage. You may also use a lap theater made from a box. (To create a lap theater, see the directions on page 36 in the "Billy Goat Adventures" storytime.)

MUSIC

Five Little Speckled Frogs

(see discography for tune)

Five little speckled frogs,
Sat on a speckled log,
Eating some most delicious bugs—yum-yum!   (*Rub tummy*)
One jumped into the pool,
where it was nice and cool,
And then there were four little speckled frogs.
Glub, glub . . .

(*Repeat until no frogs left*)

Additional Songs

You'll find more frog songs on the CD *Sing-A-Longs for Kids, Volume 1* from Time-Life Music such as "Frog Went A-Courtin'," and "A-Goong Went the Little Green Frog."

CRAFT: PET ROCK FROG

Obtain some round rocks. Rivers or streams are good places to look. Put them on newspapers outside and spray-paint them green. You'll only need to spray the tops. The natural color of the rocks will be fine for the underbelly. Let the children glue on wiggle eyes and craft foam arms and legs. Draw on smiles and spots with markers.

Supplies

Round rocks
Wiggle eyes
Craft foam
Markers
Glue

Laugh Out Loud Stories

Get ready for some giggles and laughs. You'll get a chance to enjoy some hilarious stories, shake your sillies out, act out monkeys jumping on a bed, and create a funny-looking tube puppet.

LAUGH OUT LOUD READ-ALOUDS

Alborough, Jez. *Watch Out! Big Bro's Coming*. Cambridge, MA: Candlewick, 1997.

Bond, Felicia. *Tumble Bumble*. Arden, NC: Front Street, 1996.

Feiffer, Jules. *Bark, George*. New York: HarperCollins, 1999.

Helakowski, Leslie. *Big Chickens*. New York: Dutton, 2006.

Johnson, Paul Brett. *The Goose Went Off in a Huff*. New York: Orchard Books, 2001.

_____. *Little Bunny Foo Foo: Told and Sung by the Good Fairy*. New York: Scholastic, 2004.

Nolan, Lucy. *A Fairy in the Dairy*. New York: Marshall Cavendish, 2003.

Palatini, Margie. *Oink?* New York: Simon and Schuster, 2006.

_____. *The Three Silly Billies*. New York: Simon and Schuster, 2005.

Stevens, Janet. *The Great Fuzz Frenzy*. Orlando: Harcourt, 2005.

Van Laan, Nancy. *Little Baby Bobby*. New York: Knopf, 1996.

FINGERPLAYS AND POEMS

Open and Shut Them

(folk rhyme)

(*Suit actions to words*)

Open and shut them,   (*Hold hands up, palms out*)
Open and shut them,
Give a little clap.
Open and shut them,
Open and shut them,
Put them in your lap.

Creep them, creep them,
Creep them, creep them,
Right up to your chin.
Open up your little mouth
But do not let them in!   (*Quickly put hands behind back*)

Five Little Monkeys

(folk rhyme)

Five little monkeys jumping on the bed.   (*Pretend to jump on bed*)
One fell off and bumped his head.   (*Tap forehead with fingers*)
Mama called the doctor and the doctor said (*Pretend to dial phone*)
No more monkeys jumping on the bed!!   (*Shake index finger*)

(*Repeat with 4, 3, 2, and 1.*
Last line: "Put those monkeys straight to bed!")

Monkey See, Monkey Do

(folk rhyme)

(*Suit actions to words*)

Oh when you clap, clap, clap your hands,
The monkey claps, claps, claps his hands.

Chorus:
Monkey see, monkey do.
Monkey does the same as you!

(*Repeat chorus after each of the following verses.*)

Oh when you stamp, stamp, stamp your feet . . .

Oh when you jump, jump, jump up high . . .

Oh when you turn yourself around . . .

(Idea: Have an assistant do the actions
with a monkey puppet.)

FLANNELBOARD STORY

Monkey Face

Monkey Face by Frank Asch is out of print and may be hard to find as a reference. *Bread and Honey* by Asch is essentially the same story except the character is a bear. You can use this book as a reference if you can't find *Monkey Face*. In the story a monkey draws a picture of his mother in school, and on the way home he bumps into several different animals who suggest changes to his picture. As you tell the story, add the changes to the monkey (owl eyes, rabbit ears, alligator teeth, elephant's trunk, lion's mane, and giraffe's neck) to create a very funny-looking creature. All the pieces should be made of felt to ensure they stick to one another.

MUSIC

Perform the actions in Raffi's song "Shake My Sillies Out." You can find this song on his CD *More Singable Songs.* Some other great selections are on the *Best of Silly Songs* CD from Walt Disney Records.

CRAFT: SILLY PAPER TUBE PUPPETS

Decorate paper tubes to create funny-looking creatures. Use wiggle eyes of different sizes. Make big noses and ears using paper or pom-poms. Use different kinds of craft materials and be as creative as you like.

Supplies

Paper tubes

Glue

Construction paper

Wiggle eyes

Pom-poms

Fuzzy fake fur of different colors

Markers

Any other fun craft materials you have around

Lion's mane

Owl eyes

Elephant's trunk

Giraffe's neck

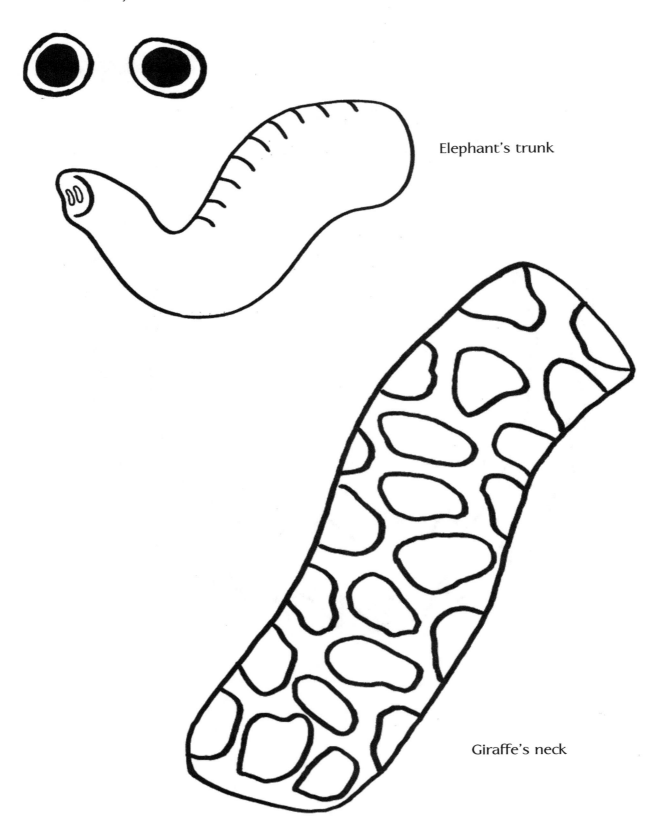

Alligator teeth

Rabbit ears

Let's Dance

Twirl and spin or get down and get funky. Do the Hokey Pokey or shake your sillies out. This storytime is full of fun and frolic. If you choose to read *Color Dance* by Ann Jonas, play some background music such as "Waltz of the Flowers," which is a selection on the CD *The Classical Child at the Ballet.* After the story, provide the children with some colorful scarves and let them dance.

DANCE READ-ALOUDS

Arnold, Marsha Diane. *Prancing, Dancing Lily.* New York: Dial, 2004.

Cronin, Doreen. *Wiggle.* New York: Atheneum, 2005.

Hager, Sarah. *Dancing Matilda.* New York: HarperCollins, 2005.

Harter, Debbie. *The Animal Boogie.* New York: Barefoot Books, 2000.

Heidbreder, Robert. *Drumheller Dinosaur Dance.* Tonawanda, NY: Kids Can Press, 2004.

Helldorfer, Mary Claire. *Got to Dance.* New York: Doubleday, 2004.

Holabird, Katharine. *Angelina Ballerina.* (Series) Middleton, WI: Pleasant Company.

Jonas, Ann. *Color Dance.* New York: Greenwillow, 1989.

LaPrise, Larry. *The Hokey Pokey.* New York: Simon and Schuster, 1997.

Schaefer, Carole Lexa. *Full Moon Barnyard Dance.* Cambridge, MA: Candlewick, 2003.

Wheeler, Lisa. *Hokey Pokey: Another Prickly Love Story.* New York: Little, Brown, 2006.

Wilson, Karma. *Hilda Must Be Dancing.* New York: Margaret K. McElderry, 2004.

Young, Amy. *Belinda the Ballerina.* New York: Viking, 2002.

FINGERPLAYS AND POEMS

Penny Thumbkin

(folk rhyme)

Penny Thumbkin upstairs,	(*Move thumbs upward*)
Penny Thumbkin down,	(*Move thumbs below shoulders*)
Penny Thumbkin dancing,	(*Dance thumbs*)
All around the town.	
Dancing on my shoulders,	(*Dance thumbs on shoulders*)
Dancing on my head,	(*Dance thumbs on head*)
Dancing on my knees now,	(*Dance thumbs on knees*)
Tuck them into bed.	(*Tuck thumbs under arms*)

(*Repeat with: Pointer finger, Tall finger,
Ring finger, Pinky finger, Family is*)

Leaves in the Wind

(*Suit actions to words*)

Dance and twirl together
Like leaves in windy weather
Twirling, swirling
We all fall down.

Ring around the Rosie

(nursery rhyme)

Ring around the rosie,
A pocket full of posies
Ashes, ashes
We all fall down!

DANCE ACTIVITIES

Here We Go Looby Loo

(traditional; see discography for tune)

(Join hands and go around in a circle; suit actions to words)

Here we go looby loo
Here we go looby light
Here we go looby loo
All on a Saturday night.
You put your right hand in
You take your right hand out
You give your hand a shake, shake, shake
And turn yourself about.

(Repeat with: left hand, right foot, left foot, whole self)

Hokey Pokey

(traditional; see discography for tune)

(Form a circle and suit actions to words)

You put your right hand in
You take your right hand out
You put your right hand in
And shake it all about,   *(Shake)*
You do the Hokey Pokey   *(Wiggle)*
And you turn yourself about,   *(Turn around)*
That's what it's all about.

(Repeat with: left hand, right foot, left foot, whole self)

MUSIC

Play Hap Palmer's CD *Walter the Waltzing Worm*. This collection of songs is designed for moving and dancing, and the songs are easy to follow. Two of the songs featured are "Song about Slow, Song about Fast" and "Swing, Shake, Twist, and Stretch." Also a lot of fun is "Shake My Sillies Out" on Raffi's CD *More Singable Songs*. In addition, you'll find "The Silly Dance Contest" on Jim Gill's CD *Jim Gill Sings the Sneezing Song and Other Contagious Tunes*. Play "Waltz of the Flowers" on the CD *The Classical Child at the Ballet* with the story *Color Dance* and let the children do a dance with colorful scarves.

CRAFT: GLITTERING DANCERS

Enlarge and trace the patterns and cut them out. Glue them onto a sheet of construction paper. Decorate them with crayons, and glue on pieces of colored tissue paper and glitter.

Supplies

Paper
Glue sticks
Glitter
Colored tissue paper
Crayons or markers

Marvelous Mud and Beasty Baths

Revel in mud and frolic in the bubbles. Decorate your story area with bath toys like rubber duckies and toy boats. Display small plastic tubs filled with fake suds (stuffing). Put various stuffed animals or puppets in the tubs. Bring out pictures of pigs in mud or other muddy scenes. Play Raffi's song "Bathtime" and blow lots of bubbles with a bubble wand. Finally, enjoy making a delicious "mud pudding."

MUD AND BATHTIME READ-ALOUDS

Knutson, Kimberley. *Muddigush.* New York: Macmillan, 1992.

Munsch, Robert. *Mud Puddle.* Toronto: Annick, 1982.

Neubecker, Robert. *Beasty Bath.* New York: Orchard, 2005.

Palatini, Margie. *Oink?* New York: Simon and Schuster, 2006.

Pelletier, Andrew Thomas. *The Amazing Adventures of Bathman.* New York: Dutton, 2005.

Puttock, Simon. *Squeaky Clean.* Boston: Little, Brown, 2002.

Ray, Mary Lyn. *Mud.* San Diego: Harcourt, 1996.

Shannon, Terry Miller. *Tub Toys.* Berkeley, CA: Tricycle Press, 2002.

Slangerup, Erik Jon. *Dirt Boy.* Morton Grove, IL: Albert Whitman, 2000.

Stewart, Amber. *Rabbit Ears.* New York: Bloomsbury, 2006.

Van Laan, Nancy. *Scrubba Dub.* New York: Atheneum, 2003.

Wolcott, Patty. *The Marvelous Mud Washing Machine.* New York: Random House, 1991.

Wood, Audrey. *King Bidgood's in the Bathtub.* New York: Harcourt, 1985.

FINGERPLAYS AND POEMS

Here Is the Baby

Here is the baby ready for his bath	(*Hold up index finger*)
Here is his little tub	(*Cup hands together*)
Put him in with all the bubbles	
And wash him rub-a-dub-dub	(*Pretend to wash finger*)
Now it's time to get him dry	(*Pretend to dry finger*)
Don't let him get away	
Now put the baby into bed	(*Open palm and place finger on it*)
Now rock-a-baby bye . . .	(*Rocking motion*)

Bubbles

This is the way we blow our bubbles	
Blow, blow, blow	(*Hold out imaginary bubble wand and blow*)
This is the way we break our bubbles	
Oh! Oh! Oh!	(*Clap hands*)

This Is the Way . . .
(folk rhyme)

(*Suit actions to words*)
This is the way we wash our hands,
Wash our hands, wash our hands,
This is the way we wash our hands,
So early in the morning.

(*Repeat with hair, knees, back, etc.;
ask children for suggestions*)

Rub-a-Dub-Dub
(Mother Goose)

Rub-a-dub-dub
Three men in a tub,
And who do you think they be?
The butcher, the baker, the candlestick-maker —
Scrub their heads knaves all three!

FLANNELBOARD POEM

Marvelous Mud

Mud, mud, marvelous mud,
There was a boy who loved to jump in the mud.
He jumped and jumped and did not stop,
And then a little puppy jumped right in on top.

They jumped and they rolled, they were quite a sight,
Until the mommy came and cried: "Oh what a fright!"
She said, "Get in the tub right this minute!"
So the dog and the boy decided to quit it.

They got in the tub,
And they were soaped, scrubbed, and rubbed.
"Don't scrub so hard, Mom," the little boy said,
But she went right on scrubbing and then soaped up his head.

When bath time was over they were shiny and clean,
But a little while later they both could be seen,
Jumping right into the marvelous mud,
The boy and his puppy, how they did love mud.

Directions

Make the standing boy and puppy figures reversible. You will need a clean side and a muddy side. Use brown fabric paint to dirty up the reverse sides of the figures. When the figures are placed in the mud, flip them over to show their muddy side. During the bath scene replace the standing figures with the boy and puppy in the tub. On "shiny and clean" remove the tub and replace it with the clean standing figures. At the end return the boy and puppy to the mud puddle. (Tip: To avoid having to memorize the poem, photocopy it and tape it to the side of your flannelboard where it can't be seen.)

MUSIC

You'll find "Rubber Duckie," "Bubble on My Snuffle," and many other bath songs on *Splish Splash,* a CD from Sony Wonder. Raffi sings "Bathtime" on his CD *Everything Grows,* and Joanie Bartels's CD *Bathtime Magic* features songs such as "There's a Hippo in My Tub" and "You Can Never Go Down the Drain." "I Like Dirt" is on the CD *Noisy Songs for Noisy Kids* by the Thunderlords, and "Why Can't Dirt Just Leave Me Alone?" is on the CD *More Songs from Jim Henson's Bear in the Big Blue House.*

CRAFT/SNACK: MUD PUDDING

Fill small bowls or cups halfway with chocolate instant pudding. Supervise the children as you let them sprinkle crushed Oreo cookies on top using a spoon. Let them decorate their treat with gummy worms or gummy bugs. Enjoy this marvelous, muddy treat! Yum!

Supplies

Pudding
Crushed Oreos
Gummy worms

Mud

Mitten Weather

Thumbs in the thumb-place, fingers all together. . . ." Brrr . . . it's cold out there. Decorate your story area with snowmen, snowflakes, and stuffed animals dressed in mittens, scarves, and hats. Introduce the storytime with a puppet that is shivering from the cold. Ask the children to tell you what kind of clothes you should put on the puppet to warm it up. Have a selection of clothing to make the puppet cozy.

MITTEN WEATHER READ-ALOUDS

Brett, Jan. *The Mitten: A Ukrainian Folktale*. New York: Putnam, 1989.

Christiansen, Candace. *The Mitten Tree*. Golden, CO: Fulcrum Kids, 1997.

Cook, Lisa Broadie. *Martin MacGregor's Snowman*. New York: Walker, 2003.

Denslow, Sharon Phillips. *In the Snow*. New York: Greenwillow, 2005.

Ehlert, Lois. *Snowballs*. San Diego: Harcourt Brace, 1995.

Fleming, Denise. *The First Day of Winter*. New York: Henry Holt, 2005.

Ford, Bernette G. *First Snow*. New York: Holiday House, 2005.

George, Kristine O'Connell. *One Mitten*. New York: Clarion, 2004.

Henkes, Kevin. *Oh!* New York: Greenwillow, 1999.

Inkpen, Mick. *Kipper's Snowy Day*. San Diego: Harcourt Brace, 1996.

Kirk, Daniel. *Snow Dude*. New York: Hyperion, 2004.

Lareau, Kara. *Snowbaby Could Not Sleep*. New York: Little, Brown, 2005.

Mahoney, Daniel. *A Really Good Snowman*. New York: Clarion, 2005.

Thompson, Lauren. *Mouse's First Snow*. New York: Simon and Schuster, 2005.

FINGERPLAYS AND POEMS

The Mitten Song

(traditional)

"Thumbs in the thumb-place,	(*Hold up thumbs*)
Fingers all together!"	(*Hold up four fingers of each hand*)
This is the song	
We sing in mitten-weather.	(*Wave hands*)
When it is cold,	(*Hold self and shiver*)
It doesn't matter whether	(*Shake head*)
Mittens are wool,	
Or made of finest leather.	
This is the song	
We sing in mitten-weather:	
"Thumbs in the thumb-place,	
Fingers all together!"	

Dancing Snowflakes

(tune: "Frère Jacques")

(*Tell the children to dance like snowflakes.
Repeat song as many times as you like.*)

Snowflakes dancing, snowflakes dancing,
In the air, everywhere,
Gently twirling snowflakes, lovely little snowflakes,
Twirling here, whirling there.

I'm a Little Snowman

(folk rhyme; tune: "I'm a Little Teapot")

I'm a Little Snowman	
Short and fat	
Here is my broomstick	(*Pretend to hold broomstick*)
Here is my hat	(*Pretend to put hat on head*)
When the sun comes out I melt away	(*Place arms in a circle overhead*)
Down, down, down, down, I'm a puddle.	(*Gradually slump down to the floor*)

Chubby Little Snowman

(folk rhyme)

A chubby little snowman had a carrot for a nose.

Along came a bunny and what do you suppose?

That hungry little bunny was looking for his lunch . . .

And he ATE that snowman's carrot nose . . . nibble, nibble . . . CRUNCH.

FLANNELBOARD POEM

Hey, Mr. Snowman

I went walking
Through a winter wonderland
And spied a frosty snowman
Who needed a hand.
Hey, Mr. Snowman, what do you need?
I need some eyes. Put them on me.
Hey, Mr. Snowman, what do you see?
I see an orange carrot. Put it on me.
Hey, Mr. Snowman, now what do you see?
I see a purple hat. Put it on me.
Hey, Mr. Snowman, now what do you see?
I see some red licorice. Put it on me.
Hey, Mr. Snowman, now what do you see?
I see some brown sticks. Put them on me.
Hey, Mr. Snowman, now what do you see?
I see a green scarf. Put it on me.
Hey, Mr. Snowman, now what do you see?
I see some red mittens. Put them on me.
Hey, Mr. Snowman, now what do you see?
I see some black buttons. Put them on me.
Hey, Mr. Snowman, now what do you see?
I see some yellow boots. Put them on me.
Hey, Mr. Snowman, now what do you see?
I see the coolest snowman ever. Me!

Directions

Place the items on the snowman as you recite the poem. The orange carrot is, of course, the nose. The red licorice and brown sticks are the mouth and arms. The children will probably want you to do this more than once. You may want to let individual children participate by letting them place the items on the board as you recite.

MUSIC

Play or sing songs from the CD *Sing a Song of Seasons* by Rachel Buchman. The winter songs on this CD are "The Mitten Song," "On a Cold and Frosty Morning," "Let's Play in the Snow," and "Mystery of the White Things."

CRAFT: SNOW PEOPLE DOILIES

Glue white paper doilies to black construction paper to form snowman shapes and decorate with interesting craft products such as glitter, sequins, eyes, beads, or buttons.

Supplies

White doilies
Construction paper (for background, scarves, mittens, hats, etc.)
Glue sticks
Wiggle eyes
Glitter
Buttons
Beads
Sequins

The Moon and Stars

These stories and songs will make you glow like the moon and twinkle like the stars. Enjoy telling the story *Moonkey* on the flannelboard and help the children create a beautiful glittering moon and star mobile.

MOON AND STARS READ-ALOUDS

Asch, Frank. *Moongame.* New York: Simon and Schuster, 1987.

Carle, Eric. *Papa, Please Get the Moon for Me.* New York: Simon and Schuster, 1986.

Conrad, Donna. *See You Soon, Moon.* New York: Knopf, 2001.

Henkes, Kevin. *Kitten's First Full Moon.* New York: Greenwillow, 2004.

Ichikawa, Satomi. *Nora's Stars.* New York: Philomel, 1988.

Jossa, Isabelle. *Ned Goes to Bed.* Vancouver: Simply Read Books, 2005.

Oliver, Jeffers. *How to Catch a Star.* New York: Philomel, 2004.

Spinelli, Eileen. *Rise the Moon.* New York: Dial, 2003.

Wallace, Nancy Elizabeth. *The Sun, the Moon, and the Stars.* Boston: Houghton Mifflin, 2003.

Yorinks, Arthur. *Quack!* New York: Abrams, 2003.

FINGERPLAYS AND POEMS

Twinkling Stars

(traditional)

At night I see the twinkling stars   (*Make twinkling motion with hand*)
And a great big smiling moon   (*Form arms in circle overhead*)
My mommy tucks me into bed   (*Pretend to tuck*)
And sings a goodnight tune.

(*Now sing "Twinkle, Twinkle, Little Star."*)

Big Yellow Moon

(folk rhyme)

Big yellow moon shines so bright,   (*Arms above head in circle shape*)
Glides across the starry night,   (*Arms move from left to right*)
Looks down at me   (*Hand shades eyes*)
Asleep in bed,   (*Hands together at side of face*)
Whispers, "Good night, sleepyhead."   (*Forefinger in front of mouth*)
Big yellow moon, your turn is done.   (*Arms above head move down in front
          of body*)

Here comes Mr. Morning Sun.   (*Arms move above head in circle shape*)
I wake up.   (*Arms stretch out*)
You go to bed.   (*Hands together at side of face*)
"Sleep well, Moon, you sleepyhead."   (*Forefinger in front of mouth*)

Moon Zoom

Zoom, zoom, I'm off to the moon!   (*Slide hands together*)
Do you want to take a trip with me?   (*Fly hands upward*)
Climb aboard my rocket ship   (*Pretend to climb a ladder*)
And with a zoom, zoom, zoom   (*Slide hands*)
We're off to the moon!

Star Light, Star Bright

(nursery rhyme)

Star light, star bright,
First star I see tonight,
I wish I may, I wish I might,
Have the wish I wish tonight.

I See the Moon
(nursery rhyme)

I see the moon,
The moon sees me.
God bless the moon,
And God bless me.

FLANNELBOARD STORY

Moonkey

Moonkey by Mike Thaler is the story of a monkey who loves the moon. His animal friends help him get to the moon in a most unusual way. Obtain a copy of the book and learn the story. Tell the story using the flannelboard figures and watch the fascination on the children's faces. Display a copy of the book.

Directions

Place the monkey on the palm tree and put up the different phases of the moon. According to the story, place the animals on top of the tree and on top of each other to help the monkey get to the moon. Repeat the process when they help the monkey get down again.

MUSIC

Twinkle, Twinkle, Little Star
(traditional)

Twinkle, twinkle, little star,
How I wonder what you are.
Up above the world so high,
Like a diamond in the sky.
Twinkle, twinkle, little star,
How I wonder what you are!

When the blazing sun is gone,
When he nothing shines upon,
Then you show your little light,
Twinkle, twinkle, all the night.
Twinkle, twinkle, little star,
How I wonder what you are!

Then the traveler in the dark
Thanks you for your tiny spark;
He could not see which way to go,
If you did not twinkle so.
Twinkle, twinkle, little star,
How I wonder what you are!

"Dad Caught Stars" and "Last Night the Moon Was Full" can be found on the CD *Not Naptime* by Justin Roberts. Also the CD *Baby's Bedtime* by Judy Collins features "Stars," "I See the Moon," and "Twinkle, Twinkle, Little Star."

CRAFT: GLITTERY MOON AND STAR MOBILE

Cut moon and star shapes from construction paper. Draw details such as a face for the moon. Add silver and gold glitter. Cross two dowels and tape in place. Tie pieces of string to the dowels. Glue the glittery stars and moon to the strings.

Supplies

Construction paper
Markers
Glue sticks
Glitter
Dowels, tape, and string

Cake

Phases
of the
moon

125

Moose on the Loose

E njoy stories about these majestic, noble, and charming creatures. Perform a marriage ceremony for a moose and a cow on the flannelboard. The flannelboard poem "Moose in Love" is based on a true story of a moose that came out of the woods into a cow pasture in Shrewsbury, Vermont. Brent Holmes has produced a DVD and a CD both entitled *Moose Tunes for Kids.* Play one of these during the moose antlers craft activity.

MOOSE READ-ALOUDS

Allen, Jonathan. *Mucky Moose.* New York: Macmillan, 1991.

Balan, Bruce. *The Moose in the Dress.* New York: Crown, 1991.

Beck, Andrea. *Elliot Gets Stuck.* Toronto: Kids Can Press, 2002.

Guthrie, Arlo. *Mooses Come Walking.* San Francisco: Chronicle, 1995.

Haseley, Dennis. *The Invisible Moose.* New York: Dial, 2006.

Lindenbaum, Pija. *Bridget and the Moose Brothers.* New York: R&S, 2004.

Numeroff, Laura Joffe. *If You Give a Moose a Muffin.* New York: HarperCollins, 1997.

Porter, Sue. *Moose Music.* New York: Artists and Writers Guild, 1994.

Waddell, Martin. *What Use Is a Moose?* Cambridge, MA: Candlewick, 1996.

West, Colin. *Moose and Mouse.* Boston: Kingfisher, 2004.

Wilson, Karma. *Moose Tracks.* New York: Margaret K. McElderry, 2006.

FINGERPLAYS AND POEMS

I'm a Moose

Look at me! I'm a moose so big and tall.	(*Stand up tall on tiptoes*)
Look at my antlers, they reach for the sky.	(*Place hands above head like antlers*)
Look at my large nose. It's lovely, Oh my!	(*Point to nose*)
Look at me, I'm a moose.	(*Point to self*)
I'm wonderful and tall!	(*Stand up tall*)

I Can Walk Like a Moose

(*Suit actions to words*)

I can walk like a moose.
I can wave my antlers around.   (*Place hands above head like antlers
and wave around*)

I can trot like a moose
And wave my big nose around.
And now I can sit right back down
On the ground.

FLANNELBOARD POEM

Moose in Love

A moose came out of the woods one day
And into a pasture of cows
He spied a young cow named Jessica
And all he could say was, "Wow!"

The moose fell in love with Jessica
And asked her to be his bride.
Jessica said to the moose, "You silly old goose!
Why, I'd love to be by your side."

So they dressed all in their finery
And got an old barn owl named Bill
To come and perform the ceremony
Under the moon, way up on a hill.

Said the moose, "O Jessica!
What a beautiful heifer you are."
Jessica said to the moose, "You elegant goof!
You're the world's sweetest moose by far!"

So hand in hand, to the tune of a band,
They got married by the light of the moon.

Directions

Make a hill from a large piece of felt. Put the hill on the board before you begin.
Place the moose and the cow on the board at the beginning of the poem. On

"dressed all in their finery" put the wedding clothes on the animals. Place all the figures on top of the hill when they marry. Put the moon on the board at the end of the poem.

Note: I was inspired to write this poem by the true story of a bull moose and a Hereford cow named Jessica. Pat Wakefield wrote a book about them called *A Moose for Jessica*. One day a moose emerged from the Vermont woods and took a liking to a cow named Jessica. My parents live near where this took place so while I was visiting them, we took a trip to Shrewsbury, Vermont, to see the lovelorn moose. When we arrived, there he was, snuggling up to Jessica. The loving antics of the moose drew quite a crowd of tourists. The moose stayed for seventy-six days and returned to the woods from whence he came.

MUSIC/GAMES

Sing or play a recording of "I'm Proud to Be a Moose" from the CD *American Children* from Alacazar Productions. For more activities take a look at *If You Give a Moose a Muffin* (book and cassette) published by HarperCollins, 1997. In addition to the story, you'll find a song called "Doin' the Moose" and a game called "The Muffin Game." Brent Holmes also has a CD and a DVD of moose songs called *Moose Tunes for Kids.*

CRAFT: MOOSE ANTLERS

Use heavy stock paper to create moose antlers. If parents are available, ask them to help cut out the antler shapes, which may be made by tracing hands. The antlers will then be taped to a headband also made of heavy stock paper. Ask parents to size the band to their child's head, remove the band, and then staple it.

Supplies

Heavy stock paper (any color)
Scissors
Staplers
Tape
Pencils

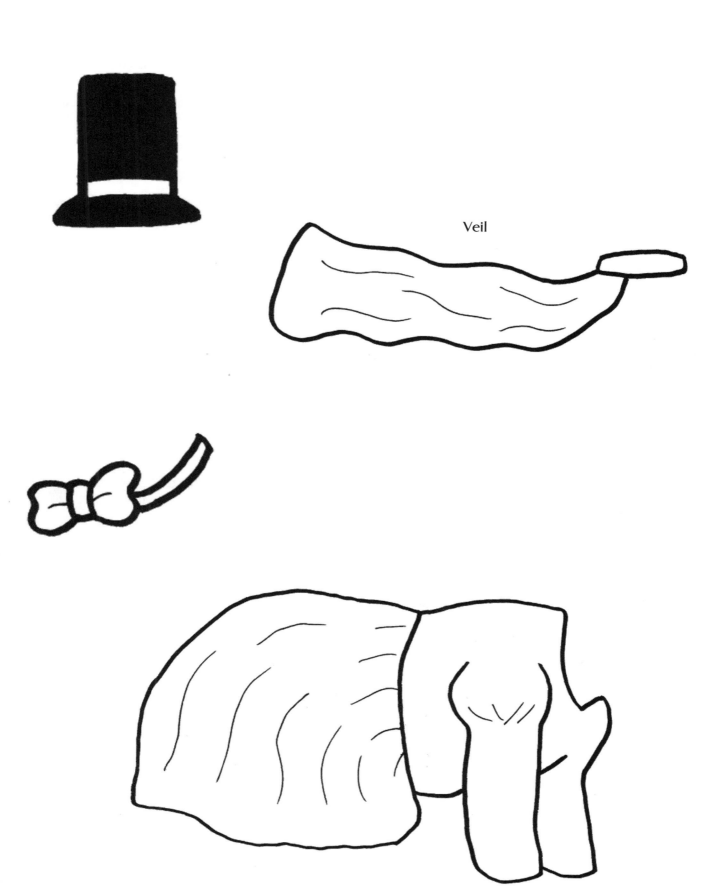

Veil

Mysterious, Magical Eggs

ll kinds of things are hatching in these "eggs"traordinary stories. Enjoy egg songs and activities and help the kids create their own Eggberts to take home.

EGG READ-ALOUDS

Brown, Margaret Wise. *The Golden Egg Book.* New York: Golden Books, 2004.

Burg, Sarah Emmanuelle. *One More Egg.* New York: North-South, 2006.

Chen, Zhiyuan. *Guji, Guji.* La Jolla, CA: Kane/Miller, 2004.

Dunbar, Joyce. *Eggday.* New York: Holiday House, 1999.

Dunrea, Oliver. *Ollie.* New York: Houghton Mifflin, 2003.

Heine, Helme. *The Most Wonderful Egg in the World.* New York: Atheneum, 1983.

Lionni, Leo. *The Extraordinary Egg.* New York: Scholastic, 1995.

Montes, Marisa. *Egg-napped.* New York: HarperCollins, 2002.

Robertson, M. P. *The Egg.* New York: Puffin, 2000.

Ross, Tom. *Eggbert, the Slightly Cracked Egg.* New York: Putnam, 1994.

Waddell, Martin. *It's Quacking Time.* Cambridge, MA: Candlewick, 2005.

Ziefert, Harriet. *This Little Egg Went to Market.* New York: Puffin, 2003.

FINGERPLAYS AND POEMS

I'm a Little Birdie

(tune: "I'm a Little Teapot")

I'm a little birdie	*(Crouch down as if inside egg)*
In my shell	
Trying to crack it open	
Peck, peck, scratch!	*(Pecking motion)*
When I crack it open,	
Out I'll pop.	*(Pop up)*
And spread my wings	*(Hands in armpits and flap)*
And tweet, tweet, tweet.	

Ten Fluffy Chickens

(folk rhyme)

Five eggs and five eggs	
That makes ten.	*(Hold up ten fingers)*
Sitting on top is Mother Hen.	*(Place fist on top of palm)*
Cackle, cackle, cackle	*(Clap three times)*
What do I see?	
Ten fluffy chickens,	*(Hold up ten fingers)*
As yellow as can be.	

Hickety, Pickety, My Black Hen

(Mother Goose)

Hickety, pickety, my black hen,
She lays eggs for gentlemen.
Sometimes nine,
Sometimes ten,
Hickety, pickety, my black hen.

Humpty Dumpty

(Mother Goose)

Humpty Dumpty sat on a wall,
Humpty Dumpty had a great fall.
All the king's horses,
And all the king's men,
Couldn't put Humpty together again.

FLANNELBOARD POEM

Ten Little Eggs

There are ten little eggs
And what do we see
They're about to crack open
"My goodness me,"
Said Mother Hen.

The first egg cracks open
And what do we see
It's a fuzzy, little duckling
Looking at me.

The second egg cracks open
And what do we see
It's a little purple dinosaur
Looking at me.

The third egg cracks open
And what do we see
It's a little turkey gobbler
Looking at me.

The fourth egg cracks open
And what do we see
It's a little, fuzzy owl
Looking at me.

The fifth egg cracks open
And what do we see
It's a funny, little platypus
Looking at me.

The sixth egg cracks open
And what do we see
It's a pretty, little bluebird
Looking at me.

The seventh egg cracks open
And what do we see
It's a snappy, little alligator
Looking at me.

The eighth egg cracks open
And what do we see
It's a long-necked ostrich
Looking at me.

The ninth egg cracks open
And what do we see
It's a little, green turtle
Looking at me.

The tenth egg cracks open
And what do we see
It's a little, yellow chicken
Looking at me.

"My baby!"
Said the mother hen,
As happy as can be.

"Mommy!" said the chick.
"Did you meet all my sisters and
   brothers?"
"What!" shrieked Mother Hen,
"My goodness me."

Directions

Make ten cracked egg tops and bottoms using the pattern. Glue the egg bottoms to the bottoms of the baby animals. Before reciting the rhyme place all the eggs on the flannelboard. Be sure the animals are covered by the shells. Remove the top part of each egg on cue according to the rhyme and reveal the secret creature inside.

MUSIC

You'll find the song "Eggbert, the Easter Egg" on the CD *Happy Easter Songs* from Sony Music. Play this song during the craft activity. *Wee Sing Dinosaurs* features the song "Eggs."

CRAFT: EGGBERT

Using plastic Easter eggs, design your own Eggbert. Glue on wiggle eyes; a red felt beret or craft hat; paper, felt, or foam arms and legs; and a pom-pom nose. Have parents help draw on mouths with a permanent marker or glue on black construction paper smiles. Put a treat inside.

Supplies

Plastic Easter eggs
Glue
Wiggle eyes
Small beret-shaped pieces of red felt
Paper, felt, or foam for arms and legs
Pom-poms
Markers

Never Smile at a Crocodile

These stories and activities are full of "SNAP!" Watch out, monkeys! Introduce the stories with a crocodile puppet. If you have some monkey finger puppets, let the croc gobble them up. Play the ever-popular Australian croc song "Never Smile at a Crocodile" to set the ambience.

CROC READ-ALOUDS

Bedford, David. *The Copy Crocs*. Atlanta: Peachtree, 2004.

Chen, Zhiyuan. *Guji, Guji*. La Jolla, CA: Kane/Miller, 2004.

Christelow, Eileen. *Five Little Monkeys Wash the Car*. New York: Clarion, 2000.

Freedman, Claire. *Where's Your Smile, Crocodile?* Atlanta: Peachtree, 2001.

Jorgensen, Gail. *Crocodile Beat*. New York: Bradbury, 1989.

Lakin, Patricia. *Beach Day!* New York: Dial, 2004.

Sayre, April Pulley. *Crocodile Listens*. New York: Greenwillow, 2001.

Sierra, Judy. *Counting Crocodiles*. San Diego: Harcourt, 1997.

_____. *What Time Is It, Mr. Crocodile?* Orlando: Gulliver, 2004.

Vrombaut, An. *Clarabella's Teeth*. New York: Clarion, 2003.

FINGERPLAYS AND POEMS

Five Little Monkeys

(folk rhyme)

Five little monkeys
Swinging in a tree
Teasing Mister Crocodile,
Can't catch me, can't catch me.
Along comes Crocodile,
Quiet as can be
And SNAPS that monkey
Right out of that tree!

(*Hold up hand to show five fingers*)

(*Shake one finger*)
(*Form alligator jaws with hands*)

(*Snap hands shut*)

(Repeat with 4, 3, 2, and 1. Last line:
"Oh, oh. No more monkeys swinging in a tree.")

Crocodile

(author unknown)

She sailed away on a summer day

On the back of a Crocodile.
You see, said she, he's as tame as can be
I'll ride him down the Nile.
The Croc winked his eye
As she bade them all good-bye
Wearing a happy smile.
At the end of the ride
The Lady was inside
And the smile on the Crocodile.

(*Place hands together and make a
wavy motion*)

(*Point and shake index finger*)
(*Hands together, make wavy motion*)
(*Wink*)
(*Wave good-bye*)
(*Smile*)
(*Hands together, wavy motion*)
(*Pat tummy*)
(*Point to smile and make snapping
motion with hands*)

FLANNELBOARD STORY

Have You Seen the Crocodile?

Have You Seen the Crocodile? by Colin West is the story of a group of animals who try to ascertain if a crocodile is anywhere around. Little do they know he is right under their noses.

Directions

Obtain a copy of the book and learn the story. Before telling the story, place the crocodile on the flannelboard partially hidden under the bush. Place each animal on the board in turn according to the story. At the end, remove the bush to reveal the crocodile. The animals are scared by the crocodile and run away. As each animal is removed from the flannelboard, you may want to say "The terrified parrot squawked and flew away" or "The dragonfly buzzed away at full speed." Display a copy of the book.

MUSIC

"Never Smile at a Crocodile" and "Five Little Monkeys" may be found on the CD *Six Little Ducks* from Kimbo Educational. "Crocodile Rock" is on the CD *Kids Rock Too* by Mr. Al.

CRAFT: SNAPPING CROCODILE

Using green paper cut out a crocodile shape from a top view. Next, fold another green piece of paper in half and cut out a pair of jaws (that fit the body) with the fold being at the back of the mouth. Let the children glue the lower jaw to the body (leaving the top of the jaw open) and glue on little paper teeth and wiggle eyes. Draw on other details with crayons or markers.

Supplies

Construction paper
Glue sticks
Wiggle eyes
Paper teeth
Markers

Penguin Power

They're frosty, stoic, well dressed, and adorable. Use a penguin puppet to introduce the storytime. Waddle around while you play the dance song "Penguin Polka," which is featured on the CD *Dance and Sing!* Have fun presenting the penguin flannelboard poems and enjoy creating a cute penguin craft.

PENGUIN READ-ALOUDS

Apperley, Dawn. *Flip and Flop.* New York: Orchard, 2001.

Cuyler, Margery. *Please Say Please! Penguin's Guide to Manners.* New York: Scholastic, 2004.

Jeffers, Oliver. *Lost and Found.* New York: Philomel, 2006.

Karas, G. Brian. *Skidamarik: A Silly Love Song to Sing Together.* New York: HarperFestival, 2002.

Kimmel, Elizabeth Cody. *My Penguin Osbert.* Cambridge, MA: Candlewick, 2004.

Lester, Helen. *Tacky and the Winter Games.* Boston: Houghton Mifflin, 2005.

Richardson, Justin. *And Tango Makes Three.* New York: Simon and Schuster, 2005.

Wiesmuller, Dieter. *The Adventures of Marco and Polo.* New York: Walker, 2000.

Wood, A. J. *The Little Penguin.* New York: Dutton, 2001.

FINGERPLAYS AND POEMS

I'm a Little Penguin

(folk rhyme)

I'm a little Penguin
And I like to waddle   (*Waddle with legs straight and arms folded under*)

And when I'm in the water
I paddle, paddle, paddle   (*Do paddling motion with arms folded*)
I jump off big rocks   (*Jump*)
Into the sea
And I swim so fast   (*Swimming motion*)
You'll never catch me!

There Was a Little Penguin

(adapted from "There Was a Little Turtle" by Vachel Lindsay)

There was a little penguin
Who went for a walk,   (*Walk like a penguin*)
Then he dived in the ocean,   (*Perform diving motion*)
And he climbed on some rocks!   (*Pretend to climb*)
He snapped at a fishy,   (*Clap hands*)
He snapped at an eel,   (*Clap hands*)
He snapped at an octopus,   (*Clap hands*)
Oh, what a meal!

FLANNELBOARD POEMS

Five Perky Penguins

Five perky penguins stood on the shore
One went for a swim and then there were four.
Four perky penguins looked out to sea
One went swimming and then there were three.
Three perky penguins said, "What can we do?"
One jumped in the water and then there were two.
Two perky penguins sat in the sun
One swam off and then there was one.
One perky penguin said, "This is no fun!"
He dived into the water and then there were none.

Five Little Penguins

Five little penguins as happy as could be
Standing on a rock, looking out at the sea.
Crash! went the waves, oh, what a din!
Said the first little penguin, "Shall we jump in?"
Said the second little penguin, "The water's like ice."
Said the third little penguin, "That's not so nice!"
Said the fourth little penguin, "Let's bask in the sun."
Said the fifth little penguin, "Hey, that's no fun!"
So the five little penguins took a leap and a dive
And splashed in the water, 1, 2, 3, 4, 5.
Three seconds later, out they popped
And stood once again atop that big rock.

Directions

Place the penguins on the flannelboard in turn and remove them according to the rhymes.

MUSIC

"The Penguin Polka" may be found on the CD *Dance and Sing! The Best of Nick Jr.* "A Rock Hopper Penguin" is on the CD *Come Dance by the Ocean* by Ella Jenkins, and you'll find "Penguins" on the CD *Fingerplays and Footplays* by Rosemary Hallum.

CRAFT: PAPER CUP PENGUIN

Purchase black paper cups from a party store or cover regular paper cups with black construction paper. Let the children glue on wiggle eyes, paper beaks, wings, feet, and a white oval tummy. Add a red bow tie if you like or even an elastic string and wear the penguin as a hat!

Supplies

Black paper cups
Black, white, and yellow construction paper
Glue
Wiggle eyes

Pizza, Pizza, Pizza!

There is fun and frolic and toppings galore in this plethora of pizza stories. Delight in performing the action rhymes, "Pizza, Pizza, Pizza!" and "Pizza Man, Pizza Man," as you throw imaginary dough into the air, put on the toppings, and slide the pizza into the oven. Make a "Pizza the Size of the Sun" on the flannelboard as you recite the poem by Jack Prelutsky from the book of the same title. The pizza craft will whet everyone's appetite for the final phase of the program . . . the pizza snack!

PIZZA READ-ALOUDS

Arnold, Ted. *Huggly's Pizza.* New York: Scholastic, 2000.

Gelman, Rita Golden. *Pizza Pat.* New York: Random House, 1999.

Hao, K. T. *One Pizza, One Penny.* Chicago: Cricket, 2003.

Holub, Joan. *The Pizza That We Made.* New York: Viking/Puffin, 2001.

Kim, Byung-Gyu. *The 100th Customer.* New York: Purple Bear, 2005.

Pelham, David. *Sam's Pizza* (pop-up). New York: Dutton, 1996.

Pienkowski, Jan. *Pizza! A Yummy Pop-Up.* Cambridge, MA: Candlewick, 2001.

Steig, William. *Pete's a Pizza.* New York: HarperCollins, 1998.

Sturges, Philemon. *The Little Red Hen Makes a Pizza.* New York: Dutton, 1999.

Walter, Virginia. *Hi, Pizza Man!* New York: Orchard, 1995.

MUSICAL ACTION RHYME

Pizza, Pizza, Pizza!

(tune: "Peanut Butter and Jelly")

(*Suit actions to words*)

Chorus:
Pizza, pizza, pizza, with cheese!
Pizza, pizza, pizza, with cheese!

(*Repeat chorus after each of the following verses.*)

First you take the dough and you knead it,
You knead it, you knead it, knead it, knead it. Singing . . .

Next you take the dough and you throw it,
You catch it, you throw it up high, singing . . .

Then you take the sauce and you spread it,
You spread it, you spread it on the pizza, singing . . .

Then you take the cheese and you sprinkle it,
You sprinkle it, you sprinkle it on the pizza, singing . . .

Next you take the toppings and you plunk 'em,
You plunk 'em, you plunk 'em on the pizza, singing . . .

Then you take the pizza and you bake it,
You bake it, you bake it in the oven, singing . . .

And when the pizza's done you eat it!
Yum, Yum!

ACTION RHYME

Pizza Man, Pizza Man

(*Suit actions to words*)

Pizza man, pizza man, turn around.
Pizza man, pizza man, touch the ground.

Pizza man, pizza man, give the dough a toss.
Pizza man, pizza man, ladle on the sauce.

Pizza man, pizza man, sprinkle the cheese.
Pizza man, pizza man, shake your bootie.

Pizza man, pizza man, put it in the oven.
Pizza man, pizza man, press the oven button.

Pizza man, pizza man, rub your tummy.
Pizza man, pizza man, eat some pizza. Yummy!

FLANNELBOARD ACTIVITY

Recite the poem "A Pizza the Size of the Sun" by Jack Prelutsky from the book of the same title. Increase the size of the patterns to a scale that works well with your flannelboard. Make the pizza and sun out of felt. They should be the same size and quite large. Make five or six of each topping piece. These should be made of felt also to decrease the chance of pieces falling off the board. You may want to add small pieces of Velcro to the back of the toppings for extra sticking power.

MUSIC

Sing or play a recording of one or more of these pizza songs: "Pepperoni Pizza" from the CD *Dr. Jean Sings Silly Songs,* "Pizza Pie Song" from the CD *Disney Silly Songs,* "Pizza Pizzazz" from the CD of the same name by Peter and Ellen Allard, or "I Am a Pizza" from the CD *Party in the Park.*

CRAFT: PIZZA

Make pizza using white paper plates. Give the children red markers or crayons to color on the sauce. Provide them with glue sticks, short pieces of yellow yarn (cheese), and precut toppings (optional).

Supplies

Paper plates
Red markers or crayons
Glue sticks
Yellow yarn
Precut pizza toppings (optional)

SNACK: PIZZA

If you have the facilities, provide a pizza snack. Make English muffin pizzas or order large pizzas cut up in small pieces.

Pizza crust

Pizza toppings

Pumpkin Time

These stories will put you in the mood to go frolicking in pumpkin patches by the light of the moon. Perform *The Halloween Pumpkin* by Pamela Oldfield as a stick puppet play. Act out *Big Pumpkin* by Erica Silverman. Sing pumpkin songs and help the children to create pumpkin masks so they can scare the living daylights out of everyone.

PUMPKIN READ-ALOUDS

Brown, Margaret Wise. *The Fierce Yellow Pumpkin.* New York: HarperCollins, 2003.

Cuyler, Margery. *The Bumpy Little Pumpkin.* New York: Scholastic, 2005.

Hubbell, Will. *Pumpkin Jack.* Morton Grove, IL: Albert Whitman, 2000.

Minor, Wendell. *Pumpkin Heads!* New York: Blue Sky, 2000.

Ochiltree, Dianne. *Sixteen Runaway Pumpkins.* New York: Margaret K. McElderry, 2004.

Rockwell, Anne. *Pumpkin Day, Pumpkin Night.* New York: Walker, 1999.

Rohmann, Eric. *Pumpkinhead.* New York: Knopf, 2003.

Silverman, Erica. *Big Pumpkin.* New York: Aladdin, 1992.

Sloat, Teri. *Patty's Pumpkin Patch.* New York: Putnam, 1999.

Wallace, Nancy Elizabeth. *Pumpkin Day!* New York: Marshall Cavendish, 2002.

Walton, Rick. *Mrs. McMurphy's Pumpkin.* New York: HarperFestival, 2004.

FINGERPLAYS AND POEMS

Orange Pumpkin

(tune: "Twinkle, Twinkle, Little Star")

Pumpkin, pumpkin orange and round, (*Stretch arms out and form a circle*)
Sitting in the pumpkin patch on the ground. (*Crouch down*)
Once you were a seed so small, (*Pretend to hold a seed*)
Now you are a great orange ball! (*Make huge circle with hands*)
Pumpkin, pumpkin orange and round, (*Stretch arms out and form a circle*)
Rolling, rolling on the ground. (*Make rolling motion with arms*)

Pumpkin Song

(folk rhyme; tune: "I'm a Little Teapot")

I'm a little pumpkin
Fat and round. (*Hold arms out to indicate roundness*)
Sitting in a pumpkin patch, (*Squat down*)
On the ground.
I can be a jack-o-lantern
With two big eyes (*Circle eyes with fingers*)
Or made into a big fat pie. (*Make pie shape with arms*)

Five Little Pumpkins

(folk rhyme)

Five little pumpkins sitting on a gate,
The first one said, "Oh, my it's getting late!"
The second one said, "There are witches in the air."
The third one said, "But we don't care."
The fourth one said, "Let's run, let's run!"
The fifth one said, "Isn't Halloween fun?"
Then Woooooo went the wind
And OUT went the lights.
And five little pumpkins rolled out of sight.

DRAMATIC PLAY

Retell the story *Big Pumpkin* by Erica Silverman while the children act it out. Have a big pumpkin available and ask the children to pretend they are trying to pull it off the vine as they line up behind each other according to the story. Assign parts to all the children who want to play. Create extra characters if you need to or assign more than one mummy or vampire or so forth so all are included.

PUPPET SHOW

The Halloween Pumpkin Stick Puppet Lap Theater Play

The Halloween Pumpkin by Pamela Oldfield is the story of a jack-o-lantern who goes about scaring people and yelling, "OO-AH! OO-AH!" When he encounters a huge pig, he finally meets his match. This story makes a particularly good stick puppet play because, in the book, the pumpkin is actually on a stick. He gets around by bumping along on the stick, which makes him a little scary but also funny.

Obtain a copy of the book and learn the story. Use the patterns to create stick puppets for use in a lap theater. (To create a lap theater, see the directions on page 36 in the "Billy Goat Adventures" storytime. The puppet patterns are located at the end of this section.)

MUSIC

The *Wee Sing for Halloween* CD has plenty of pumpkin songs such as "Pumpkin, Pumpkin" and "Carving Pumpkins." The *Spooky Favorites* CD from Music for Little People features "Five Little Pumpkins" and "Jack-o-Lantern."

CRAFT: PUMPKIN MASK

To prepare for the craft, cut eyeholes in orange paper plates or in round, orange shapes of heavy stock paper. Create mouths and noses with black construction paper and add green stems. Use yarn for hair if desired or use other interesting craft materials to decorate the pumpkin. Tape on craft sticks to serve as holders. Have fun scaring each other.

Supplies

Orange paper plates
Black and green construction paper
Glue sticks
Craft sticks
Yarn or other craft materials (optional)

Purr-fect Cats

"T"he smallest feline is a masterpiece" (Leonardo da Vinci). Enjoy an abundance of cool cats with purr power in these great stories and help the children create a cat mask to take home.

PURR-FECT READ-ALOUDS

Baker, Keith. *Cat Tricks.* San Diego: Harcourt, 1997.

Capucilli, Alyssa Satin. *Little Spotted Cat.* New York: Dial, 2005.

Day, Nancy Raines. *A Kitten's Year.* New York: HarperCollins, 2000.

Duncan, Lois. *I Walk at Night.* New York: Puffin, 2002.

Gay, Marie-Louise. *Caramba.* Berkeley, CA: Group West, 2005.

Henkes, Kevin. *Kitten's First Full Moon.* New York: Greenwillow, 2004.

Jewel, Nancy. *Five Little Kittens.* New York: Clarion, 1999.

Kuskin, Karla. *So, What's It Like to Be a Cat?* New York: Atheneum, 2005.

Saltzberg, Barney. *I Love Cats.* Cambridge, MA: Candlewick, 2005.

Schachner, Judith Byron. *The Grannyman.* New York: Dutton, 1999.

FINGERPLAYS AND POEMS

Little Kittens

(folk rhyme)

Five little kittens   *(Hand made into a fist)*
All fluffy and white
Sleeping and purring
All through the night.
It's time to get up now sleepyheads.
Meow, meow, meow, meow, meow   *(Each finger raised in turn to "meow")*
Five little kittens all up from their beds.

Little Mousie

(folk rhyme)

Here's a little mousie,
Peeking through a hole,   *(Poke index finger of one hand*
                              through fist of the other hand)

Peek to the left,   *(Wiggle finger to the left)*
Peek to the right,   *(Wiggle finger to the right)*
Pull your head back in,   *(Pull finger into fist)*
There's a cat in sight!

Five Little Kittens

(folk rhyme)

Five little kittens, sleeping on a chair
One rolled off, leaving four there.
Four little kittens, one climbed a tree
To look in a bird's nest; then there were three.
Three little kittens, wondered what to do.
One saw a mouse; then there were two.
Two little kittens, playing in the hall.
One little kitten chased a red ball.
One little kitten, with fur soft as silk,
Was left all alone to drink a dish of milk.

(May be used with the flannelboard.)

Pussycat, Pussycat

(nursery rhyme)

Pussycat, pussycat, where have you been?
I've been to London to visit the Queen.
Pussycat, pussycat, what did you there?
I frightened a little mouse under her chair.

(Act out with puppets.)

FLANNELBOARD STORY

Scat the Cat

(author unknown)

Once there was a cat named Scat. Scat had a beautiful coat of soft black fur. One day he noticed that all his brothers and sisters also had black fur. So Scat decided he wanted to be different. He wanted to change his color.

He said, "I'm Scat the Cat. I'm sassy and fat and I can change my color just like that!" (Snap fingers.)

All of a sudden Scat turned blue just like the water, the sky, and blueberry pie. Then Scat walked to a pond to admire his reflection. But he was there only a minute when he slipped and fell into the water! He called for help but his friends couldn't see him because he was blue just like the water. Finally, a kindly turtle pulled him to shore. He was one wet cat and Scat decided that he didn't want to be blue anymore.

So he said, "I'm Scat the Cat. I'm sassy and fat. I can change my color just like that!" (Snap fingers.)

All of a sudden he turned green like the grass, the trees, grasshoppers, and frogs. It was easy for Scat to be green—that is, until he went out to play with his friends. His friends couldn't find him because he matched the grass so well he blended right in to it and could not be seen. So his friends played without him. Now Scat the Cat was very unhappy and lonely and he didn't want to be green and unseen anymore.

So he said, "I'm Scat the Cat. I'm sassy and fat and I can change my color just like that!" (Snap fingers.)

In a flash Scat turned yellow like the sun, lemons, and Easter chicks. Later when he was walking through the zoo, Scat met a lion. The lion was jealous of Scat's shiny yellow coat and said, "Roar! I'm the only cat who is supposed to be yellow!" The lion scared Scat. He was so scared that he wanted to change his color again.

So he said, "I'm Scat the Cat. I'm sassy and fat and I can change my color just like that!" (Snap fingers.)

This time Scat turned bright red like a candied apple, fire engines, and licorice. Scat was finally sure he was the best color in the world and he went out to play with his friends. But they all made fun of him and laughed and said, "Who ever heard of a red cat?" Scat felt sad and a little mad and decided he didn't want to be fire engine red anymore. He didn't want to be yellow like a lemon. He didn't want to be blue like the sky, and he didn't want to be green like the trees. He just wanted to be himself again.

So he said, "I'm Scat the Cat. I'm sassy and fat and I can change my color just like that!" (Snap fingers.)

So Scat changed back to black and after that, he was quite happy just being himself.

Directions

Use the pattern to make a cat of each color. To set the scene, place a blue piece of felt shaped like a pond and a green piece for grass on the flannelboard. When Scat falls into the water, cover him with the pond. Put him behind the grass when he turns green. To encourage participation during the story, ask the children to name other things that are blue, green, yellow, and red.

MUSIC

Three Little Kittens

(Mother Goose; see discography for tune)

Three little kittens,
They lost their mittens,
And they began to cry,
Oh, Mother dear,
We sadly fear
Our mittens we have lost.
What! Lost your mittens,
You naughty kittens!
Then you shall have no pie.
Mee-ow, mee-ow, mee-ow, mee-ow.
You shall have no pie.

The three little kittens,
They found their mittens,
And they began to cry,
Oh, Mother dear,
See here, see here,
Our mittens we have found.
What! Found your mittens,
You darling kittens!
Then you shall have some pie.
Mee-ow, mee-ow, mee-ow, mee-ow.
You shall have some pie.

The three little kittens,
Put on their mittens,
And soon ate up the pie;
Oh, Mother dear,
We greatly fear
Our mittens we have soiled.
What! Soiled your mittens,
You naughty kittens!
Then they began to sigh,
Mee-ow, mee-ow, mee-ow, mee-ow.
They began to sigh.

The three little kittens,
They washed their mittens,
And hung them out to dry;
Oh Mother dear,
Look here, look here,
Our mittens we have washed.
What! Washed your mittens,
You're such good kittens.
I smell a rat close by!
Hush! Hush! Hush! Hush!
Hush! Hush! Hush!
I smell a rat close by.

Activity

Play a recording of "Three Little Kittens." Select children to do the actions, while you play the role of the mother cat. You will need three pairs of mittens, a washtub or basin, a small clothesline, clothespins, and a pie. (Use a pie tin and felt to make an imitation pie.) Act out the poem as many times as you like, giving all the children a chance to participate.

CRAFT: CAT MASKS

Create masks using paper plates. To prepare the craft, cut eyeholes in the plates. Tape craft sticks onto the plates so they can be held up to the face. Use different craft materials to create the face such as pipe cleaner whiskers, construction paper ears, pom-pom noses, and colored tissue paper for spots or fur color. (Participation: Use the masks to act out "Three Little Kittens.")

Supplies

Paper plates
Glue
Craft sticks
Construction paper
Colored tissue paper
Pipe cleaners
Pom-poms

169

Snuggle Stories

nvite your audience to wear their pj's and bring teddy bears to this storytime. They'll enjoy snuggling up to their teddies and listening to stories and lullabies that are guaranteed to give them sweet dreams. Help them create glow worms to take home.

SNUGGLE READ-ALOUDS

Brown, Margaret Wise. *Goodnight, Moon.* New York: HarperCollins, 2005.

Dewdney, Anna. *Llama, Llama Red Pajama.* New York: Viking, 2005.

Doyle, Malachy. *One, Two, Three O'Leary.* New York: Margaret K. McElderry, 2005.

Fore, S. J. *Tiger Can't Sleep.* New York: Viking, 2006.

Freedman, Claire. *Snuggle Up, Sleepy Ones.* Intercourse, PA: Good Books, 2005.

Jones, Sally Lloyd. *Time to Say Goodnight.* New York: HarperCollins, 2006.

Lewis, Kim. *Good Night, Harry.* Cambridge, MA: Candlewick, 2004.

Markes, Julie. *Shhhhh! Everybody's Sleeping.* New York: HarperCollins, 2005.

Peck, Jan. *Way Up High in a Tall Green Tree.* New York: Simon and Schuster, 2005.

Puttock, Simon. *Earth to Stella.* New York: Clarion, 2006.

Thompson, Lauren. *Little Quack's Bedtime.* New York: Simon and Schuster, 2005.

FINGERPLAYS AND POEMS

This Little Girl

(folk rhyme)

This little girl is ready for bed.   (*Hold up index finger*)
Down on the pillow she lays her head.   (*Put finger in palm*)
She wraps herself in the covers tight,   (*Close hand over finger*)
And this is the way she sleeps all night.

Teddy Bear Dance

(*Suit actions to words*)

Dance with your teddy up on your toes,
Swing your little teddy there he goes,
Hug your little teddy hold him tight,
Kiss your little teddy and say goodnight.

Here Is the Baby

(folk rhyme)

Here is the baby ready for a nap.   (*Hold up index finger*)
Lay him down in his mother's lap.   (*Place index finger on palm*)
Cover him up so he won't peep.   (*Close hand over finger*)
Rock him 'til he's fast asleep.   (*Rock hands back and forth*)

Ten in the Bed

(traditional)

There were ten in the bed   (*Hold up two hands with fingers extended*)
And the little one said,   (*Wiggle a pinkie*)
Roll over, Roll over!   (*Make fists and roll arms*)
So they all rolled over
And one fell out.
There were nine in the bed   (*Hold up two hands with nine fingers extended*)
                                                         (*Repeat until . . .*)

There was one in the bed,
and the little one said,
Good Night!

FLANNELBOARD STORY

Lisa Can't Sleep

Lisa Can't Sleep by Kaj Beckman is the story of a little girl who puts so many toys in her bed there is no room left for her. The cumulative nature of the story makes for a very charming flannelboard presentation.

Directions

Obtain a copy of the book and learn the story. Place each toy on the bed in turn according to the story; remove them at the end and then place Lisa and her doll on the bed. Display a copy of the book.

MUSIC

You will find wonderful sleepy time songs on the CD *Lullabies for Little Dreamers* from Kid Rhino. *Lullaby Classics: A Concert for Little Ears* from Buena Vista Records is another great selection.

CRAFT: GLOW WORMS

String glow-in-the-dark beads on pipe cleaners. Fold one end of the pipe cleaner into a small ball to form a head. Glue on wiggle eyes. Fold the tail end of the pipe cleaner to hold the beads in place. The children will enjoy seeing their "glow worms" glow in the dark when they go to bed.

Supplies

Pipe cleaners
Glow-in-the-dark beads
Glue
Wiggle eyes

Squirrel Tales

"This is a tale about a tail—a tail that belonged to a little red squirrel, and his name was Nutkin" (Beatrix Potter). Enjoy these stories about our little bushy-tailed friends. Play "Little Squirrel Came Home" on the CD *The Library Boogie* by Tom Knight and help the children create lunch-bag squirrels to take home.

SQUIRREL READ-ALOUDS

Bynum, Janie. *Nutmeg and Barley: A Budding Friendship.* Cambridge, MA: Candlewick, 2006.

Chichester Clark, Emma. *Will and Squill.* Minneapolis: Carolrhoda, 2006.

Cooper, Helen. *A Pipkin of Pepper.* New York: Farrar, Straus and Giroux, 2005.

_____. *Pumpkin Soup.* New York: Farrar, Straus and Giroux, 1999.

Ehlert, Lois. *Nuts to You.* San Diego: Harcourt Brace Jovanovich, 1993.

Freeman, Don. *Earl the Squirrel.* New York: Viking, 2005.

Pfister, Marcus. *Hopper's Treetop Adventure.* New York: North-South, 1997.

Potter, Beatrix. *The Tale of Squirrel Nutkin.* New York: Frederick Warne, 1903.

Shore, Diane ZuHone. *Look Both Ways: A Cautionary Tale.* New York: Bloomsbury, 2005.

FINGERPLAYS AND POEMS

This Little Squirrel
(folk rhyme)

This little squirrel said, Let's run and play.	(*Point to each finger in turn*)
This little squirrel said, Let's hunt nuts today.	
This little squirrel said, Yes, nuts are good.	
This little squirrel said, Yes, they are our best food.	
This little squirrel said, Come climb this tree	(*Hold up arm with open hand to represent tree, run fingers up it*)
And crack these nuts, one, two, three.	(*Clap hands*)

This Is the Squirrel
(folk rhyme)

This is the squirrel	(*Stick thumb up*)
Hunting for nuts,	
This is the hole	(*Make a hole with thumb and index finger of your other hand*)
Where day by day	
Nut after nut	
He stores away.	(*Pretend to place nuts in hole with thumb*)
When winter comes	
With its cold and storm	
He'll sleep curled up,	(*Cover squirrel with other hand*)
All snug and warm.	

FLANNELBOARD POEMS

Five Squirrels
(folk rhyme)

Five little squirrels sitting in a tree.
The first one said, "It's getting cold for me."
The second one said, "The leaves are falling to the ground."
The third one said, "Let's get busy, there's nuts to be found."
The fourth one said, "We better not wait."
The fifth one said, "Fall is really great!"

Five Little Squirrels

Five little squirrels playing in the sun,
The first little squirrel said, "Isn't this fun!"
The second little squirrel said, "I see a bear."
The third little squirrel said, "Let's run away from here."
The fourth little squirrel said, "Let's hide in the shade."
The fifth little squirrel said, "I'm not afraid."
Then "Growl!" went the bear and away they all ran,
Right up the tree!

Directions

Use the tree pattern from the "Apple of My Eye" storytime on page 13. Place each squirrel on the flannelboard on cue as you recite the rhymes. When the bear appears in the second rhyme, put the squirrels in the tree.

ACTIVITY

Acorn Search

Hide acorns around the room and ask the children to search for them. Talk about how squirrels gather acorns for the winter and store them in their nests.

MUSIC

You'll find "Grey Squirrel" on the CD *Baby-O!* by Mary Lee Sunseri. "Little Squirrel Came Home" is on the CD *The Library Boogie* by Tom Knight.

CRAFT: LUNCH-BAG SQUIRREL

Stuff a brown lunch bag with shredded paper. Do not pack it. Seal the bag with tape. With the help of parents, let the children tie ribbons around the bags to form a neck. Draw on a face and whiskers. Add wiggle eyes and a pom-pom nose. Glue on paper arms, legs, and ears. Attach a big pinecone to the back for a tail or, if you don't have pinecones, create tails with craft fake fur.

Supplies

Brown bags	Pom-poms
Shredded paper or stuffing	Wiggle eyes
Glue	Construction paper
Tape	Pinecones or craft fur
Markers	

Up, Up, and Away: Beautiful Balloons

Learn how to create simple animal balloons by referring to the books suggested in the section "Balloon Activity." The children will be dazzled by your skills. If you want even more balloon fun, help the children and parents create miniature hot air balloons using helium balloons and paper cups.

BALLOON READ-ALOUDS

Baker, Alan. *Brown Rabbit's Shape Book.* New York: Kingfisher, 1994.

Bynum, Janie. *Altoona Baboona.* San Diego: Harcourt, 1999.

Calhoun, Mary. *Hot-Air Henry.* New York: William Morrow, 1981.

Curtis, Jamie Lee. *Where Do Balloons Go? An Uplifting Mystery.* New York: HarperCollins, 2000.

DeBeer, Hans. *Little Polar Bear and the Big Balloon.* New York: North-South, 2002.

Delacre, Lulu. *Nathan's Balloon Adventure.* New York: Scholastic, 1991.

Dematons, Charlotte. *The Yellow Balloon.* Asheville, NC: Front Street, 2003.

Hayes, Sarah. *The Grumpalump.* New York: Clarion, 1991.

Nolen, Jerdine. *Harvey Potter's Balloon Farm.* New York: Lothrop, Lee, and Shepard, 1993.

FINGERPLAYS AND POEMS

Red Balloon

(folk rhyme)

Here's my great big red balloon	(*Indicate round shape with hands*)
I'll blow it up one, two, three	(*Pretend to blow up a balloon*)
Not too much air will it take	(*Shake finger back and forth*)
Or pop!	(*Clap hands*)
No more balloon for me.	

I Love Balloons

I love balloons, yes I do
Yellow, red, purple, or blue
I love colors pretty and bright.
I love orange, green, and white.
I don't want my balloon to sail away
So I'll hold it tight
All through the day.

BALLOON ACTIVITY

There are many books, such as *The Ultimate Balloon Book: 46 Projects to Blow Up, Bend and Twist* by Shar Levine, which have simple step-by-step instructions for creating animal balloon sculptures. It's not difficult to make these sculptures, and the children will love watching you create them during the program. Make lots of balloon animals before the program to display in the story space. Be sure to make enough to give one to each child after the storytime. To prepare for the program, become proficient at making two or three different sculptures. Take some time during the program to make a few projects while the children watch. Tell them they may each have an animal when they leave.

Some other useful titles to inspire you are *The Great Balloon Party Book: The Do-It-Yourself Guide to Throwing Your Own Fantastic Balloon-Theme Party* by Aaron Hsu-Flanders, and *Balloon Animals* by Barb Whiter.

MUSIC

You'll find the song "Balloon-alloon-alloon" on the CD *I've Got a Yo-Yo* by Tom Paxton. "Where Do They Make Balloons" is on the CD *No!* by They Might Be Giants (musical group).

CRAFT: HOT AIR BALLOONS

Tie paper cups to helium balloons with three or four strands of ribbon or string. Parents will need to assist. The cups may be decorated beforehand. Create little people or animals to ride in the cup using construction paper. Make sure one piece of string attached to the balloon is longer so the hot air balloon can float up high. Tie the long string to the child's wrist.

Supplies

Helium balloons
Paper cups
String or ribbon
Tape
Construction paper

Valentine Cookie Monsters

Enjoy heart-warming stories and the sweetness of homemade valentine cookies. Request that the parents or caregivers bring valentine cookies to share. Play the song "All You Need Is Love" while helping the children create a heart flower craft.

VALENTINE READ-ALOUDS

Carr, Jan. *Sweet Hearts*. New York: Holiday House, 2002.

Davenier, Christine. *Leon and Albertine*. New York: Orchard, 1998.

Engelbreit, Mary. *Queen of Hearts*. New York: HarperCollins, 2005.

Karas, G. Brian. *Skidamarik: A Silly Love Song to Sing Together*. New York: HarperFestival, 2002.

London, Jonathan. *Froggy's First Kiss*. New York: Puffin, 2000.

Rylant, Cynthia. *If You'll Be My Valentine*. New York: HarperCollins, 2005.

Samuels, Barbara. *Happy Valentine's Day, Dolores*. New York: Farrar, Straus and Giroux, 2006.

Thompson, Lauren. *Mouse's First Valentine*. New York: Simon and Schuster, 2002.

Wallace, Nancy Elizabeth. *The Valentine Express*. Tarrytown, NY: Marshall Cavendish, 2004.

Weeks, Sarah. *Be Mine, Be Mine, Sweet Valentine*. New York: Laura Geringer, 2006.

FINGERPLAYS AND POEMS

Five Little Hearts

(folk rhyme)

Five little hearts,
Five little hearts all in a row.
The first one said, "I love you so."
The second one said, "Will you be my Valentine?"
The third one said, "I will, if you'll be mine."
The fourth one said, "I'll always be your friend."
The fifth one said, "We'll all be friends until the very end."

(Idea: Use heart finger puppets with this rhyme.)

My Heart Goes Thump, Thump

My heart goes thump, thump	*(Pat chest)*
And my feet jump, jump	*(Jump)*
When I see you.	*(Point to children)*
Do you know what you do	
To make my heart thump, thump	*(Pat chest)*
And my feet jump, jump?	*(Jump)*
It's all because	
I love you!	

Won't You Bee My Valentine?

(folk rhyme)

Won't you bee my Valentine?	*(Point at each other)*
And buzz away with me?	*(Pretend to buzz around)*
We'll bumble along together	
Because you're my honey bee!	
BUZZZZZZZZZZZZZZZZZ!	

FLANNELBOARD POEM

The Valentine Cookies

The cookie jar valentines
Pushed open the lid,
Climbed up the side,
And out then all slid.

They said, "Let's escape!
Let's give it a whirl!
We mustn't be eaten
By that boy or the girl!"

The first little cookie
Opened his red heart eyes
And looked all around
For a hiding place his size.

The second little cookie
All frosted in pink
Said, "What do we do now?
Let's think, think, think."

The third little cookie
With a candy heart nose
Was so happy to be free
She danced on her toes.

The fourth little cookie
Did a flip and a twist
And slid across the floor,
In a sugary mist.

The fifth little cookie
With frosted blue topping
Said, "I think all our fun
Will soon be stopping."

Because into the kitchen
Came a hungry little boy.
There was munching and crunching
And much yummy joy.

The Valentine cookies,
I'm sorry to say
Will not be seen again
Until next Valentine's Day!

Directions

Place each cookie on the board in turn according to the poem. Place the boy on the board at the end of the poem. Touch each cookie to his mouth and then palm it while making noisy chewing sounds.

MUSIC

You Are My Valentine

(tune: "You Are My Sunshine")

You are my valentine,
My funny valentine.
You make me happy
Oh yes you do.
I want you to know dear
How much I love you
Here is my heart
It is for you!

Additional Music

"All You Need Is Love" may be found on the CD *All You Need Is Love* from Music for Little People. You'll also find "The World We Love" on the CD *Bananaphone* by Raffi.

CRAFT: HEART FLOWERS

Make heart flowers using pipe cleaners for stems and construction paper hearts for flower petals. Glue one heart or more to a pipe cleaner. Glue small green hearts to the stems for leaves. Decorate the flower with more tiny heart stickers of different colors. Let the children make several each so they have enough to give away to loved ones.

Supplies

Construction paper
Glue
Pipe cleaners
Heart stickers

What a Hoot!

L et's go owling. You never know "whooo" you might meet. During this storytime you'll get a chance to sing some owl songs, present *Good-Night Owl* on the flannelboard, and show the kids how to make a beautiful feathered owl to take home.

OWL READ-ALOUDS

Allen, Jonathan. *I'm Not Cute!* New York: Hyperion, 2005.

Goldsmith, Howard. *Sleepy Little Owl.* New York: Learning Triangle, 1997.

Hendra, Sue. *Oliver's Wood.* Cambridge, MA: Candlewick, 1996.

Hissey, Jane. *Hoot.* New York: Random House, 1997.

Hutchins, Pat. *Good-Night Owl!* New York: Macmillan, 1972.

Johnston, Tony. *The Barn Owls.* Watertown, MA: Charlesbridge, 2000.

McDonald, Megan. *Whoo-oo Is It?* New York: Orchard, 1992.

Nicholls, Judith. *Billywise.* New York: Bloomsbury, 2002.

Tomlinson, Jill. *The Owl Who Was Afraid of the Dark.* Cambridge, MA: Candlewick, 2001.

Waddell, Martin. *Owl Babies.* Cambridge, MA: Candlewick, 1992.

Yolen, Jane. *Owl Moon.* New York: Philomel, 1987.

FINGERPLAYS AND POEMS

There's a Big Eyed Owl

(folk rhyme)

There's a Big Eyed Owl,	(*Join thumbs and forefingers and look through*)
With a pointed nose.	(*Point to nose*)
Two pointed ears and claws for his toes.	(*Point fingers from head and form claws with fingers*)
He sits up in a tree,	(*Point to imaginary tree*)
And he looks at you.	(*Point to children*)
He flaps his wings,	(*Flap arms*)
And says "Whooo! Whooo!"	

Five Little Owls

(folk rhyme)

Five little owls on a dark, dark night.	(*Hold up five fingers*)
Five little owls are quite a sight.	
Five little owls. Are you keeping score?	
One flies away and that leaves four.	(*Fly hand behind back and bring it back with four fingers up. Repeat the process for 3, 2, and 1.*)
Four little owls as happy as can be.	
One flies away and that leaves three.	
Three little owls calling, "Who, Who, Who!"	
One flies away and that leaves two.	
Two little owls having lots of fun.	
One flies away and that leaves one.	
One little owl and we're almost done!	
He flies away and that leaves none.	(*Hold out empty hands*)

(*Idea: Make five owls and present the poem on the flannelboard.*)

Wise Old Owl

(folk rhyme)

A wise old owl sat in an oak,
The more he heard, the less he spoke;
The less he spoke, the more he heard;
Why aren't we all like that wise old bird?

FLANNELBOARD STORY

Good-Night Owl!

Good-Night Owl! by Pat Hutchins is a story about an owl who tries to get some sleep, but many pesky birds and other animals keep him awake. Make the story figures out of felt. Make one side of each figure with eyes open and the opposite side with eyes closed. Make the owl with both eyes open on one side and one eye open on the other. (He never *did* get to sleep.) Turn the figures over to show sleep or wakefulness at appropriate times during the story. Use the tree pattern from the "Apple of My Eye" storytime on page 13.

MUSIC

On the CD *Sing A to Z* by Sharon, Lois, and Bram you will find the song "Owl Lullaby," and *Wee Sing Animals, Animals, Animals* features "One Little Owl." On the CD *100 Toddler Favorites* you will also find "The Owl and the Pussy Cat."

CRAFT: COLORFUL FEATHERED OWL

Decorate an owl shape cut from heavy stock paper with a paper beak, wiggle eyes, and colorful feathers. Attach the wings with brads if you want them to move. Glue on a craft stick so you can hold him up high and show him off.

Supplies

Heavy stock paper
Glue sticks
Wiggle eyes
Feathers
Brads
Craft sticks

Wild Things

Enjoy these wonderful books about wild animals and have a great time telling the Indian folk tale "The Tiger, the Brahman, and the Jackal." The children will be fascinated by this tale about a hungry tiger. The fun fingerplays and action rhymes are sure to release a lot of energy, and everyone will enjoy singing along to "The Lion Sleeps Tonight" and other songs while creating a paper bag lion puppet.

WILD READ-ALOUDS

Alborough, Jez. *Tall.* Cambridge, MA: Candlewick, 2005.

Ashman, Linda. *Starry Safari.* Orlando: Harcourt, 2005.

Bright, Paul. *Nobody Laughs at a Lion.* Intercourse, PA: Good Books, 2005.

_____. *Quiet!* New York: Orchard, 2003.

Fatio, Louise. *The Happy Lion.* New York: Knopf, 1982.

Fore, S. J. *Tiger Can't Sleep.* New York: Viking, 2006.

Harvey, Damian. *Just the Thing.* Columbus, OH: Gingham Dog Press, 2005.

Ireland, Karin. *Don't Take Your Snake for a Stroll.* San Diego: Harcourt, 2003.

Laird, Elizabeth. *Beautiful Bananas.* Atlanta: Peachtree, 2003.

Lillegard, Dee. *Tiger, Tiger.* New York: Putnam, 2002.

Taylor, Thomas. *The Loudest Roar.* New York: Arthur A. Levine, 2003.

FINGERPLAYS AND POEMS

Let's Hear You Roar!

Let's hear you roar like a lion!
Let's see you jump like a frog.
Let's see you snap your jaws like a crocodile.
Let's hear you howl like a dog.
Pretend you're an elephant with a big, long trunk.
Pretend you're a monkey, let's see you jump, jump, jump.
And now you're a mouse . . . Just let me see
How very, very quiet you can be.

Five Little Monkeys

(folk rhyme)

Five little monkeys   *(Hold up hand to show five fingers)*
Swinging in a tree
Teasing Mister Alligator,
Can't catch me, can't catch me.
Along comes Mister Alligator,   *(Form alligator jaws with hands)*
Quiet as can be
And SNAPS that monkey   *(Snap hands shut)*
Right out of that tree!

*(Repeat with 4, 3, 2, and 1. Last line:
"Oh, oh. No more monkeys swinging in a tree.")*

The Spotted Giraffe

(folk rhyme)

The spotted giraffe is as tall as could be   *(Hold arm up high)*
His lunch is a bunch of leaves off a tree   *(Make a nibbling motion with fingers)*
He has a very long neck   *(Point to neck)*
And his legs are long too.   *(Point to legs)*
And he can run much faster,
Than his friends at the zoo.

DRAMATIC PLAY

Reread *The Loudest Roar* by Thomas Taylor as the children act it out. Use as many animal characters as you need so everyone gets a chance to play. Let the children perform the roars and sound effects.

FLANNELBOARD STORY

The Tiger, the Brahman, and the Jackal (A Tale from India)

Long ago and far away, in the country of India, a tiger found himself caught in a trap. He roared and raged and tried to break out through the bars . . . but he could not. By chance, a Brahman, a holy man, walked by.

The tiger pleaded with him and begged to be let out of the cage. The Brahman thought about it and said: "Tiger, if I let you out of this cage you will swallow me in one gulp. I'd have to be crazy to do a foolish thing like that. And you must be very hungry having been trapped for such a long while."

The tiger replied: "Oh, no. All I want is my freedom. I promise I won't harm a hair on your head if you set me free."

The Brahman had a soft heart. By his nature he wanted to help others. So . . . he let the tiger out.

The tiger popped out of the cage and in a flash he pounced on the Brahman and held him to the ground. "Mr. Brahman, you are indeed a fool. Now I'm going to swallow you in one gulp."

The Brahman pleaded with the tiger to have mercy on him. "I saved your life! Why do you repay me for a good deed by swallowing me? It just isn't fair. Please let me go."

"Why should I?" asked the tiger. "Didn't you know this is how it would be? I'm a ferocious tiger after all. This is what tigers do."

"I have just one request before I die. Let me talk to three others and if they believe I deserve this fate, and you are justified in eating me, I will lay myself down on your dinner plate and have no more complaints."

"Very well, but be quick about it. I'm famished."

So the Brahman went down the road and the first thing he came across was a tree. And the tree said, "Mr. Brahman, why do you look so depressed? Is anything wrong?"

"I let a tiger out of a trap and now he wants to repay me by devouring me. Do you think it is fair that I'm repaid for kindness by being eaten?"

"Well, it seems to be the way of the world now, doesn't it? Every day I provide passersby with lovely shade under my beautiful branches and how do they repay me? They tear off my leaves and branches and feed them to their cows and goats. I say, be a man and go face your fate."

The Brahman went down the road more depressed than ever. Soon the road began talking to him. "What's the matter, Mr. Brahman? You're looking a little down in the mouth. Pray tell what is bothering you?"

The Brahman told the road his tale of woe and the road said, "What are *you* complaining about? Look at me. I'm useful to everyone, but what thanks do I get? Dust kicked in my face day in and day out. People throw garbage on me and sometimes even spit on me and give not one word of thanks. Go meet your fate bravely and stop whining."

A little while later, the Brahman came upon a jackal. "Why do you look so sad, Friend?" asked the jackal. Again the Brahman told his sad tale, but Jackal couldn't understand him.

"I'm afraid I don't understand. Did you say a tiger let you out of a cage? So what's your problem?"

"No, no. I'm the one who let *him* out."

"So, now who's in the cage?"

"No one is in the cage! He's going to eat me!!!"

"I'm afraid I'm all mixed up. I think you'll have to show me what happened. Then maybe I'll understand."

So the Brahman took Jackal back to the tiger.

"Oh, here comes lunch and an appetizer too!" the tiger gleefully whispered to himself when he saw them approaching.

When they got there the Brahman began to explain, "Tiger, I need to explain to Jackal here how it came to be that you are out of your cage. You see, Jackal, this is the cage I found the tiger in and . . ."

"Oh, I see . . . the tiger found the cage and tried to put you in it so you wouldn't eat him."

"No, no, no . . . You idiot!" growled the tiger. "Let me show you. When Brahman walked by I was in the cage like this." The tiger got inside the cage and shut the door.

"Yes, now I understand. . . . You were in the cage and Mr. Brahman was not. Well, maybe that's how it should remain," said Jackal as he quickly latched the cage door before the tiger could get out.

After that Jackal and the Brahman walked on down the road and became the best of friends.

Directions

Use the tree pattern from the "Apple of My Eye" storytime on page 13. When you make the Brahman story figure, add details (face, clothing, etc.) to both sides of the figure. He will need to be reversible in order to face the jackal and tiger at different times in the story. Create a cage by gluing together strips of felt. When the tiger pounces on the Brahman, place the Brahman on his back with the tiger on top of him. Remove the tiger and cage from the board while the Brahman talks to the tree, road, and Jackal. When the Brahman talks to the road, tip him slightly forward so it looks like he is addressing the road. You may use a strip of brown felt or yarn to indicate the road.

MUSIC

You'll find "The Lion Sleeps Tonight" on the CD *Rhythm of the Pridelands: Music Inspired by the Lion King.* This song can also be found on the CD *The Lion King: Original Broadway Cast Recording.* Many other songs appropriate for this theme are on these CDs too.

CRAFT: PAPER BAG LION PUPPET

On a paper bag, draw a nose and whiskers and glue on wiggle eyes. Glue short pieces of yarn or crinkled paper shreds on the paper bag to create the mane. A piece of yarn with a frayed end glued to the back will serve as a tail. Glue on paper ears, sharp, white paper teeth, and paper arms with claws.

Supplies

Paper bags

Glue sticks

Yarn or crinkled paper

Wiggle eyes

Paper

A Woggle of Witches

I'll get you, my pretty, and your little dog too!" The witches in the books listed here are, of course, not nearly as scary as the Wicked Witch of the West. Though some are a little ill-humored, most are cute, funny, quirky, and always entertaining. Dress up as a witch or wizard and invite the children to do the same. Decorate the room with witches and cats. (Use stuffed toys if you have them.) Play a game of pass the witch's hat, sing Halloween tunes, and enjoy creating a black cat craft.

WITCH READ-ALOUDS

Adams, Adrienne. *A Woggle of Witches.* New York: Scribner, 1971.

Buehner, Caralyn. *A Job for Wittilda.* New York: Dial, 1993.

Donaldson, Julia. *Room on the Broom.* New York: Puffin, 2001.

Glassman, Miriam. *Halloweena.* New York: Atheneum, 2002.

Glassman, Peter. *My Working Mom.* New York: William Morrow, 1994.

Horn, Emily. *Excuse Me – Are You a Witch?* Watertown, MA: Charlesbridge, 2003.

Howard, Arthur. *Hoodwinked.* San Diego: Harcourt, 2001.

Krieb, Richard. *We're Off to Find the Witch's House.* New York: Dutton, 2005.

Leuck, Laura. *One Witch.* New York: Walker, 2003.

Silverman, Erica. *Big Pumpkin.* New York: Aladdin, 1992.

Somers, Kevin. *Meaner Than Meanest*. New York: Hyperion, 2001.

Spurr, Elizabeth. *Halloween Sky Ride*. New York: Holiday House, 2005.

FINGERPLAYS AND POEMS

I'm a Little Witch

(tune: "I'm a Little Teapot")

I'm a little witch with a big black cat.   (*Pretend to pet cat*)

Here is my broomstick.   (*Hold imaginary broom*)

Here is my hat.   (*Pretend to place hat on head*)

You'd better be careful.   (*Wag finger*)

You'd better beware.

'Cause I might give you a great, big scare. Boo!

Very Old Witch

(folk rhyme)

A very old witch was stirring a pot,   (*Make a stirring motion*)

Ooooooooo two little ghosts said,

What has she got?

Tippy-toe, tippy-toe, tippy-toe   (*Tip-toe*)

Booooooo!

DRAMATIC PLAY

Retell the story *Big Pumpkin* by Erica Silverman while the children act it out. Have a big pumpkin available and ask the children to pretend they are trying to pull it off the vine as they line up behind each other according to the story. Assign parts to all the children who want to play. Create extra characters if you need to or assign more than one mummy or vampire or so forth so all are included.

FLANNELBOARD POEM

Five Little Witches

Five little witches sitting on a gate.

The First one said "I'm glad it's getting late."

The Second one said "There are spiders in my hair!"

The Third one said "Well, I declare!"

The Fourth one said "Trick or treating would be fun!"
The Fifth one said "Let's run and run and run!"
So, Woooo oooo went the wind
And out went the light
And the five little witches flew out of sight!

Directions

Place the gate on the flannelboard before beginning the rhyme. Place the witches on the gate one by one on cue and remove them at the end of the poem.

GAME

Pass the Witch/Wizard Hat

Have the children sit in a circle. Play Halloween music and ask them to pass a witch/wizard hat around the circle. When the music stops whoever is holding the hat will receive a small prize or treat. Time it so that each child receives a prize or treat.

MUSIC

Halloween Witches

(folk rhyme; tune: "Ten Little Indians")

One little, two little, three little witches   (*Count out three fingers*)
Flying over haystacks   (*Fly hand up and down*)
Gliding over ditches
Slide down moonbeams without any hitches   (*Glide hand downward*)
Heigh-ho! Halloween's here!

Additional Music

You'll find witch and Halloween songs galore on the CD *Wee Sing Halloween* by Pamela Beall.

CRAFT: WITCH'S BLACK CAT

Create black cats using construction paper. The cat's body is a construction paper cone. Prepare this ahead of time using half circles of construction paper. Also cut out cat head shapes, legs, and a tail. Make enough for all program participants. The children will create the cat's face. Give them white oval shapes for the eyes that they can color with crayons and glue on. Small pink pom-poms may be glued on to make the nose and short pieces of yarn may be glued on to create whiskers. Draw the mouth with light-colored crayons. Next, glue the head to the top of the cone, legs to the body, and tail to the back. Add elastic string if you would like to make the cat into a hat.

Supplies

Black construction paper
Glue sticks
White paper for eyes
Crayons or markers
Pink pom-poms
Yarn for whiskers

Gate

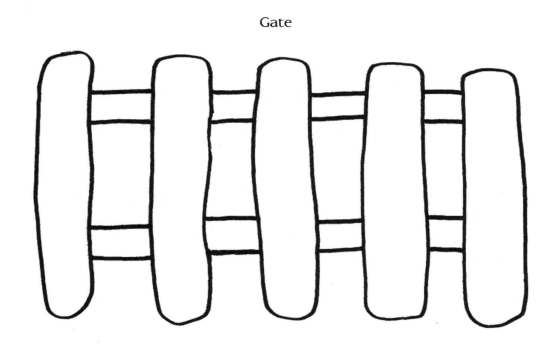

BIBLIOGRAPHY

Ada, Alma Flor. *Friend Frog.* San Diego: Harcourt, 2000.

Adams, Adrienne. *A Woggle of Witches.* New York: Scribner, 1971.

Alakija, Polly. *Catch That Goat!* Cambridge, MA: Barefoot Books, 2002.

Alborough, Jez. *Tall.* Cambridge, MA: Candlewick, 2005.

_____. *Watch Out! Big Bro's Coming.* Cambridge, MA: Candlewick, 1997.

Allen, Jonathan. *I'm Not Cute!* New York: Hyperion, 2005.

_____. *Mucky Moose.* New York: Macmillan, 1991.

Appelt, Kathi. *The Bat Jamboree.* New York: Morrow, 1996.

_____. *Bats Around the Clock.* New York: HarperCollins, 2000.

_____. *Bats on Parade.* New York: Morrow, 1999.

Apperley, Dawn. *Flip and Flop.* New York: Orchard, 2001.

Archer, Dosh. *Looking After Little Ellie.* New York: Bloomsbury, 2005.

Arnold, Marsha Diane. *Prancing, Dancing Lily.* New York: Dial, 2004.

Arnold, Ted. *Huggly's Pizza.* New York: Scholastic, 2000.

Asch, Frank. *Baby Bird's First Nest.* San Diego: Harcourt, 1999.

_____. *Bread and Honey.* New York: Parents Magazine Press, 1981.

_____. *Monkey Face.* New York: Parents Magazine Press, 1977.

_____. *Moongame.* New York: Simon and Schuster, 1987.

Asher, Sandy. *Too Many Frogs.* New York: Philomel, 2005.

Ashman, Linda. *Starry Safari.* Orlando: Harcourt, 2005.

_____. *To the Beach!* New York: Harcourt, 2005.

Aylesworth, Jim. *The Gingerbread Man.* New York: Scholastic, 1998.

Bailey, Carolyn Sherwin. *The Little Rabbit Who Wanted Red Wings.* New York: Platt and Monk, 1988.

Baker, Alan. *Brown Rabbit's Day.* New York: Kingfisher, 1995.

_____. *Brown Rabbit's Shape Book.* New York: Kingfisher, 1994.

Baker, Keith. *Cat Tricks.* San Diego: Harcourt, 1997.

Balan, Bruce. *The Moose in the Dress.* New York: Crown, 1991.

Barrett, Judi. *Animals Should Definitely Not Wear Clothing.* New York: Atheneum, 1970.

Baumgart, Klaus. *Anna and the Little Green Dragon.* New York: Hyperion, 1992.

Beaumont, Karen. *I Ain't Gonna Paint No More.* Orlando: Harcourt, 2005.

Beck, Andrea. *Elliot Gets Stuck.* Toronto: Kids Can Press, 2002.

Beckman, Kaj. *Lisa Can't Sleep.* New York: Farrar, Straus and Giroux, 1990.

Bedford, David. *The Copy Crocs.* Atlanta: Peachtree, 2004.

Berkeley, Jon. *Chopsticks.* New York: Random House, 2006.

Bertrand, Lynne. *Dragon Naps.* New York: Viking, 1996.

Blackstone, Stella. *Secret Seahorse.* Cambridge, MA: Barefoot Books, 2004.

Bond, Felicia. *Tumble Bumble.* Arden, NC: Front Street, 1996.

Bornstein, Ruth. *Rabbit's Good News.* New York: Clarion, 1995.

Bosca, Francesca. *The Apple King.* New York: North-South, 2001.

Bratun, Katy. *Gingerbread Mouse.* New York: HarperCollins, 2003.

Brett, Jan. *Gingerbread Baby.* New York: Putnam, 1999.

_____. *The Mitten: A Ukrainian Folktale.* New York: Putnam, 1989.

Bright, Paul. *Nobody Laughs at a Lion.* Intercourse, PA: Good Books, 2005.

_____. *Quiet!* New York: Orchard, 2003.

Brown, Margaret Wise. *The Fierce Yellow Pumpkin.* New York: HarperCollins, 2003.

_____. *The Golden Egg Book.* New York: Golden Books, 2004.

_____. *Goodnight, Moon.* New York: HarperCollins, 2005.

_____. *I Like Bugs.* New York: Golden Books, 1999.

_____. *The Runaway Bunny.* New York: HarperCollins, 2005.

Bruel, Nick. *Boing.* Brookfield, CT: Roaring Brook, 2004.

Buehner, Caralyn. *A Job for Wittilda.* New York: Dial, 1993.

Burg, Sarah Emmanuelle. *One More Egg.* New York: North-South, 2006.

Bynum, Janie. *Altoona Baboona*. San Diego: Harcourt, 1999.

_____. *Nutmeg and Barley: A Budding Friendship*. Cambridge, MA: Candlewick, 2006.

Cabrera, Jane. *Cat's Colors*. New York: Dial, 1997.

Calhoun, Mary. *Hot-Air Henry*. New York: William Morrow, 1981.

Cannon, Janell. *Stellaluna*. San Diego: Harcourt, 1993.

Capucilli, Alyssa Satin. *Little Spotted Cat*. New York: Dial, 2005.

Carle, Eric. *Papa, Please Get the Moon for Me*. New York: Simon and Schuster, 1986.

_____. *The Very Lonely Firefly*. New York: Philomel Books, 1995.

Carr, Jan. *Sweet Hearts*. New York: Holiday House, 2002.

Chen, Zhiyuan. *Guji, Guji*. La Jolla, CA: Kane/Miller, 2004.

Chichester Clark, Emma. *I Love You, Blue Kangaroo!* New York: Scholastic, 2001.

_____. *Will and Squill*. Minneapolis: Carolrhoda, 2006.

Chodos-Irvine, Margaret. *Best Best Friends*. Orlando: Harcourt, 2006.

Christelow, Eileen. *Five Little Monkeys Wash the Car*. New York: Clarion, 2000.

Christiansen, Candace. *The Mitten Tree*. Golden, CO: Fulcrum Kids, 1997.

Conrad, Donna. *See You Soon, Moon*. New York: Knopf, 2001.

Cook, Lisa Broadie. *Martin MacGregor's Snowman*. New York: Walker, 2003.

Cooper, Helen. *A Pipkin of Pepper*. New York: Farrar, Straus and Giroux, 2005.

_____. *Pumpkin Soup*. New York: Farrar, Straus and Giroux, 1999.

Cousins, Lucy. *Maisy Makes Gingerbread*. Cambridge, MA: Candlewick, 1999.

Cronin, Doreen. *Click, Clack, Moo: Cows That Type*. New York: Simon and Schuster, 2000.

_____. *Wiggle*. New York: Atheneum, 2005.

Curtis, Jamie Lee. *Where Do Balloons Go? An Uplifting Mystery*. New York: HarperCollins, 2000.

Cuyler, Margery. *The Bumpy Little Pumpkin*. New York: Scholastic, 2005.

_____. *Please Say Please! Penguin's Guide to Manners*. New York: Scholastic, 2004.

Davenier, Christine. *Leon and Albertine*. New York: Orchard, 1998.

Davies, Nicola. *Bat Loves the Night*. Cambridge, MA: Candlewick, 2001.

Davis, Katie. *Who Hops?* San Diego: Harcourt, 1998.

Day, Nancy Raines. *A Kitten's Year*. New York: HarperCollins, 2000.

De Regniers, Beatrice Schenk. *May I Bring a Friend?* New York: Atheneum, 1964.

DeBeer, Hans. *Little Polar Bear and the Big Balloon*. New York: North-South, 2002.

Degen, Bruce. *Daddy Is a Doodlebug*. New York: HarperCollins, 2000.

Delacre, Lulu. *Nathan's Balloon Adventure*. New York: Scholastic, 1991.

Dematons, Charlotte. *The Yellow Balloon*. Asheville, NC: Front Street, 2003.

Denslow, Sharon Phillips. *In the Snow*. New York: Greenwillow, 2005.

Dewdney, Anna. *Llama, Llama Red Pajama*. New York: Viking, 2005.

Dodd, Emma. *Dog's Colorful Day: A Messy Story about Colors and Counting*. New York: Dutton, 2000.

Dodds, Siobhan. *Grumble! Rumble!* New York: Dorling Kindersley, 2000.

Donaldson, Julia. *Room on the Broom*. New York: Puffin, 2001.

Doyle, Malachy. *One, Two, Three O'Leary*. New York: Margaret K. McElderry, 2005.

Dunbar, Joyce. *Eggday*. New York: Holiday House, 1999.

Duncan, Lois. *I Walk at Night*. New York: Puffin, 2002.

Dunrea, Oliver. *Gossie and Gertie*. Boston: Houghton Mifflin, 2002.

_____. *Ollie*. New York: Houghton Mifflin, 2003.

Edwards, Pamela Duncan. *Gigi and Lulu's Gigantic Fight*. New York: Katherine Tegen, 2004.

_____. *McGillycuddy Could!* New York: Katherine Tegen, 2005.

_____. *Ms. Bitsy Bat's Kindergarten*. New York: Hyperion, 2005.

Ehlert, Lois. *Color Farm*. New York: HarperCollins, 1997.

_____. *Color Zoo*. New York: Lippincott, 1989.

_____. *Nuts to You*. San Diego: Harcourt Brace Jovanovich, 1993.

_____. *Snowballs*. San Diego: Harcourt Brace, 1995.

Elliott, Laura. *Hunter's Best Friend at School*. New York: HarperCollins, 2002.

Engelbreit, Mary. *Queen of Hearts*. New York: HarperCollins, 2005.

Ernst, Lisa Campbell. *The Gingerbread Girl*. New York: Dutton, 2006.

Ets, Marie Hall. *Elephant in a Well*. New York: Viking, 1972.

Fanelli, Sara. *Wolf*. New York: Dial, 1997.

Fatio, Louise. *The Happy Lion*. New York: Knopf, 1982.

Faulkner, Keith. *Funny Farm: A Mix-up Pop-up Book*. New York: Scholastic, 2001.

_____. *The Wide-Mouthed Frog: A Pop-up Book*. New York: Dial, 1996.

Feiffer, Jules. *Bark, George*. New York: HarperCollins, 1999.

Finch, Mary. *The Three Billy Goats Gruff*. Cambridge, MA: Barefoot Books, 2001.

Fleming, Denise. *The First Day of Winter*. New York: Holt, 2005.

Ford, Bernette G. *First Snow*. New York: Holiday House, 2005.

Fore, S. J. *Tiger Can't Sleep*. New York: Viking, 2006.

Freedman, Claire. *Snuggle Up, Sleepy Ones*. Intercourse, PA: Good Books, 2005.

_____. *Where's Your Smile, Crocodile?* Atlanta: Peachtree, 2001.

Freeman, Don. *Corduroy Goes to the Beach*. New York: Penguin, 2006.

_____. *Earl the Squirrel*. New York: Viking, 2005.

Galdone, Paul. *The Gingerbread Boy*. New York: Clarion, 1975.

_____. *The Three Billy Goats Gruff*. New York: Clarion, 1973.

Galloway, Ruth. *Clumsy Crab*. Wilton, CT: Tiger Tales, 2005.

Gay, Marie-Louise. *Caramba*. Berkeley, CA: Group West, 2005.

Gelman, Rita Golden. *Pizza Pat*. New York: Random House, 1999.

Genechten, Guido van. *Kangaroo Christine*. Wilton, CT: Tiger Tales, 2006.

George, Kristine O'Connell. *One Mitten*. New York: Clarion, 2004.

Gibbons, Gail. *The Seasons of Arnold's Apple Tree*. San Diego: Harcourt, 1984.

Ginsburg, Mirra. *Clay Boy*. New York: Greenwillow, 1997.

Glassman, Miriam. *Halloweena*. New York: Atheneum, 2002.

Glassman, Peter. *My Working Mom*. New York: William Morrow, 1994.

Gliori, Debi. *Flora's Blanket*. New York: Orchard Books, 2001.

Goldsmith, Howard. *Sleepy Little Owl*. New York: Learning Triangle, 1997.

Gorbachev, Valeri. *Big Little Elephant*. Orlando: Harcourt, 2005.

_____. *The Big Trip*. New York: Philomel, 2004.

_____. *That's What Friends Are For*. New York: Philomel, 2005.

Greenburg, David. *Bugs!* Boston: Little, Brown, 1997.

Gugler, Laurel Dee. *There's a Billy Goat in the Garden*. Cambridge, MA: Barefoot Books, 2003.

Guthrie, Arlo. *Mooses Come Walking*. San Francisco: Chronicle, 1995.

Hager, Sarah. *Dancing Matilda*. New York: HarperCollins, 2005.

Hall, Zoe. *The Apple Pie Tree*. New York: Scholastic, 1996.

Hanel, Wolfram. *Little Elephant's Song*. New York: North-South, 2000.

Hao, K. T. *One Pizza, One Penny*. Chicago: Cricket, 2003.

Harter, Debbie. *The Animal Boogie*. New York: Barefoot Books, 2000.

Hartman, Bob. *Grumblebunny*. New York: Putnam, 2003.

Harvey, Damian. *Just the Thing*. Columbus, OH: Gingham Dog Press, 2005.

Haseley, Dennis. *The Invisible Moose*. New York: Dial, 2006.

Hayes, Sarah. *The Grumpalump*. New York: Clarion, 1991.

Heidbreder, Robert. *Drumheller Dinosaur Dance*. Tonawanda, NY: Kids Can Press, 2004.

Heide, Florence Perry. *That's What Friends Are For*. Cambridge, MA: Candlewick, 2003.

Heine, Helme. *The Most Wonderful Egg in the World*. New York: Atheneum, 1983.

Helakowski, Leslie. *Big Chickens*. New York: Dutton, 2006.

Helldorfer, Mary Claire. *Got to Dance*. New York: Doubleday, 2004.

Hendra, Sue. *Oliver's Wood*. Cambridge, MA: Candlewick, 1996.

Henkes, Kevin. *Kitten's First Full Moon*. New York: Greenwillow, 2004.

_____. *Oh!* New York: Greenwillow, 1999.

_____. *Owen*. New York: Greenwillow, 1993.

Hest, Amy. *Baby Duck and the Cozy Blanket*. Cambridge, MA: Candlewick, 2002.

Hillert, Margaret. *The Little Cookie*. Cleveland: Modern Curriculum Press, 1981.

Hissey, Jane. *Hoot*. New York: Random House, 1997.

Hoban, Tania. *Is It Red? Is It Yellow? Is It Blue? An Adventure in Color*. New York: Greenwillow, 1978.

Hoberman, Mary Ann. *Bill Grogan's Goat*. Boston: Little, Brown, 2002.

Holabird, Katharine. *Angelina Ballerina*. (Series) Middleton, WI: Pleasant Company, 2000.

Holub, Joan. *The Pizza That We Made*. New York: Viking/Puffin, 2001.

Horn, Emily. *Excuse Me – Are You a Witch?* Watertown, MA: Charlesbridge, 2003.

Howard, Arthur. *Hoodwinked*. San Diego: Harcourt, 2001.

Hsu-Flanders, Aaron. *The Great Balloon Party Book: The Do-It-Yourself Guide to Throwing Your Own Fantastic Balloon-Theme Party*. New York: McGraw-Hill, 2004.

Hubbell, Will. *Pumpkin Jack*. Morton Grove, IL: Albert Whitman, 2000.

Hunter, Jana Novotny. *Little Ones Do!* New York: Dutton, 2001.

Hutchins, Pat. *Good-Night Owl!* New York: Macmillan, 1972.

_____. *Ten Red Apples*. New York: Greenwillow, 2000.

Ichikawa, Satomi. *Nora's Stars*. New York: Philomel, 1988.

Inkpen, Mick. *Kipper's Snowy Day*. San Diego: Harcourt Brace, 1996.

Ireland, Karin. *Don't Take Your Snake for a Stroll*. San Diego: Harcourt, 2003.

Jahn-Clough, Lisa. *Alicia's Best Friends*. Boston: Houghton Mifflin, 2003.

Jeffers, Oliver. *Lost and Found*. New York: Philomel, 2006.

Jewel, Nancy. *Five Little Kittens*. New York: Clarion, 1999.

Johnson, Paul Brett. *The Goose Went Off in a Huff*. New York: Orchard, 2001.

_____. *Little Bunny Foo Foo: Told and Sung by the Good Fairy*. New York: Scholastic, 2004.

Johnston, Tony. *The Barn Owls*. Watertown, MA: Charlesbridge, 2000.

Jonas, Ann. *Color Dance*. New York: Greenwillow, 1989.

Jones, Sally Lloyd. *Time to Say Goodnight*. New York: HarperCollins, 2006.

Jorgensen, Gail. *Crocodile Beat*. New York: Bradbury, 1989.

Jossa, Isabelle. *Ned Goes to Bed*. Vancouver: Simply Read Books, 2005.

Kalan, Robert. *Jump, Frog, Jump!* New York: Greenwillow, 1981.

Karas, G. Brian. *Skidamarik: A Silly Love Song to Sing Together*. New York: HarperFestival, 2002.

Kasza, Keiko. *The Dog Who Cried Wolf*. New York: Putnam, 2005.

_____. *The Mightiest*. New York: Putnam, 2001.

_____. *Wolf's Chicken Stew*. New York: Putnam, 1987.

Keller, Holly. *Geraldine's Blanket*. New York: Harper, 1988.

Kelly, Martin. *Five Green and Speckled Frogs*. New York: Handprint, 2000.

Kent, Jack. *Joey Runs Away*. Englewood Cliffs, NJ: Prentice-Hall, 1985.

_____. *There's No Such Thing as a Dragon*. New York: Golden Press/Western, 1975.

Kim, Byung-Gyu. *The 100th Customer*. New York: Purple Bear Books, 2005.

Kimmel, Elizabeth Cody. *My Penguin Osbert*. Cambridge, MA: Candlewick, 2004.

Kirk, Daniel. *Snow Dude*. New York: Hyperion, 2004.

Kirk, David. *Miss Spider's Wedding*. New York: Scholastic, 1995.

Knudsen, Michelle. *Autumn Is for Apples*. New York: Random House, 2001.

Knutson, Kimberley. *Muddigush*. New York: Macmillan, 1992.

Krensky, Stephen. *Milo the Really Big Bunny*. New York: Simon and Schuster, 2006.

Krieb, Richard. *We're Off to Find the Witch's House*. New York: Dutton, 2005.

Kuskin, Karla. *So, What's It Like to Be a Cat?* New York: Atheneum, 2005.

Laird, Elizabeth. *Beautiful Bananas*. Atlanta: Peachtree, 2003.

Lakin, Patricia. *Beach Day!* New York: Dial, 2004.

LaPrise, Larry. *The Hokey Pokey*. New York: Simon and Schuster, 1997.

Lareau, Kara. *Snowbaby Could Not Sleep*. New York: Little, Brown, 2005.

Lester, Helen. *Hooway for Wodney Wat*. Boston: Houghton Mifflin, 1999.

_____. *Listen, Buddy*. Boston: Houghton Mifflin, 1995.

_____. *A Porcupine Named Fluffy*. Boston: Houghton Mifflin, 1986.

_____. *Tacky and the Winter Games*. Boston: Houghton Mifflin, 2005.

Leuck, Laura. *One Witch*. New York: Walker, 2003.

Levine, Shar. *The Ultimate Balloon Book: 46 Projects to Blow Up, Bend and Twist*. New York: Sterling, 2001.

Levitin, Sonia. *When Kangaroo Goes to School*. Flagstaff, AZ: Rising Moon, 2001.

Lewis, Kim. *Good Night, Harry*. Cambridge, MA: Candlewick, 2004.

Lillegard, Dee. *The Big Bug Ball*. New York: Putnam, 1999.

_____. *Tiger, Tiger*. New York: Putnam, 2002.

Lindenbaum, Pija. *Bridget and the Moose Brothers*. New York: R&S, 2004.

Lionni, Leo. *The Extraordinary Egg*. New York: Scholastic, 1995.

London, Jonathan. *Froggy's First Kiss*. New York: Viking, 1998; Puffin, 2000.

_____. *Wiggle Waggle*. San Diego: Harcourt, 1999.

Loomis, Christine. *Scuba Bunnies*. New York: Putnam, 2004.

Mahoney, Daniel. *A Really Good Snowman*. New York: Clarion, 2005.

Mallat, Kathy. *Oh, Brother*. New York: Walker, 2003.

Mann, Pamela. *The Frog Princess*. Milwaukee: Gareth Stevens, 1995.

Markes, Julie. *Shhhhh! Everybody's Sleeping*. New York: HarperCollins, 2005.

Martin, Bill. *Brown Bear, Brown Bear, What Do You See?* New York: Holt, 1992.

Massie, Diane Redfield. *The Baby Bee Bee Bird*. New York: HarperCollins, 2003.

Masurel, Claire. *Big Bad Wolf*. New York: Scholastic, 2002.

Mayhew, James. *Who Wants a Dragon?* New York: Orchard Books, 2004.

McDonald, Megan. *Whoo-oo Is It?* New York: Orchard, 1992.

McGory, Anik. *Kidogo*. New York: Bloomsbury, 2005.

McKee, David. *Elmer and the Lost Teddy*. New York: Lothrop, Lee, and Shepard, 1999.

McNaughton, Colin. *Oops!* San Diego: Harcourt, 1997.

_____. *Suddenly!* San Diego: Harcourt, 1995.

Meddaugh, Susan. *Harry on the Rocks*. Boston: Houghton Mifflin, 2003.

Meres, Jonathan. *The Big Bad Rumor*. New York: Orchard, 2000.

Milbourne, Anna. *On the Seashore*. Tulsa, OK: Usborne Books, 2006.

Miller, Virginia. *Ten Red Apples.* Cambridge, MA: Candlewick, 2002.

Minor, Wendell. *Pumpkin Heads!* New York: Blue Sky, 2000.

Mitchard, Jacquelyn. *Baby Bat's Lullaby.* New York: HarperCollins, 2004.

Monks, Lydia. *The Cat Barked?* New York: Dial, 1999.

Montes, Marisa. *Egg-napped.* New York: HarperCollins, 2002.

Moore, Maggie. *The Three Little Pigs.* Minneapolis: Picture Window, 2003.

Most, Bernard. *The Cow That Went Oink.* San Diego: Harcourt, 1990.

Munsch, Robert. *Mud Puddle.* Toronto: Annick, 1982.

_____. *The Sand Castle Contest.* New York: Scholastic, 2005.

Murphy, Jill. *Five Minutes' Peace.* New York: Putnam, 1986.

Neubecker, Robert. *Beasty Bath.* New York: Orchard, 2005.

Newton, Jill. *Gordon in Charge.* New York: Bloomsbury, 2003.

Nicholls, Judith. *Billywise.* New York: Bloomsbury, 2002.

Nolan, Lucy. *A Fairy in the Dairy.* New York: Marshall Cavendish, 2003.

Nolen, Jerdine. *Harvey Potter's Balloon Farm.* New York: Lothrop, Lee, and Shepard, 1993.

Novak, Matt. *Too Many Bunnies.* Brookfield, CT: Roaring Brook, 2005.

Numeroff, Laura Joffe. *If You Give a Moose a Muffin.* New York: HarperCollins, 1997.

Ocean Picture Pops: Amazing Photo Pop-ups Like You've Never Seen Before. New York: Priddy Books, 2005.

Ochiltree, Dianne. *Sixteen Runaway Pumpkins.* New York: Margaret K. McElderry, 2004.

Oldfield, Pamela. *The Halloween Pumpkin.* Chicago: Children's Press, 1974.

Oliver, Jeffers. *How to Catch a Star.* New York: Philomel, 2004.

O'Malley, Kevin. *Little Buggy Runs Away.* San Diego: Gulliver, 2003.

Palatini, Margie. *Oink?* New York: Simon and Schuster, 2006.

_____. *The Three Silly Billies.* New York: Simon and Schuster, 2005.

Parker, Toni Trent. *Snowflake Kisses and Gingerbread Smiles.* New York: Scholastic, 2002.

Partridge, Elizabeth. *Moon Glowing.* New York: Dutton, 2002.

Patricelli, Leslie. *Blankie.* Cambridge, MA: Candlewick, 2005.

Payne, Emmy. *Katy No-Pocket.* Boston: Houghton Mifflin, 1972.

Peck, Jan. *Way Down Deep in the Deep Blue Sea.* New York: Simon and Schuster, 2004.

_____. *Way Up High in a Tall Green Tree.* New York: Simon and Schuster, 2005.

Peek, Merle. *Mary Wore Her Red Dress.* New York: Clarion, 1985.

Peet, Bill. *The Whingdingdilly.* Boston: Houghton Mifflin, 1970.

Pelham, David. *Sam's Pizza* (pop-up). New York: Dutton, 1996.

Pelletier, Andrew Thomas. *The Amazing Adventures of Bathman.* New York: Dutton, 2005.

Perret, Delphine. *The Big Bad Wolf and Me.* New York: Sterling, 2006.

Pfister, Marcus. *Hopper's Treetop Adventure.* New York: North-South, 1997.

Pienkowski, Jan. *Pizza! A Yummy Pop-Up.* Cambridge, MA: Candlewick, 2001.

Porter, Sue. *Moose Music.* New York: Artists and Writers Guild, 1994.

Potter, Beatrix. *The Tale of Squirrel Nutkin.* New York: Frederick Warne, 1903.

Prelutsky, Jack. *A Pizza the Size of the Sun: Poems.* New York: Greenwillow, 1996.

Puttock, Simon. *Big Bad Wolf Is Good.* New York: Sterling, 2002.

_____. *Earth to Stella.* New York: Clarion, 2006.

_____. *Squeaky Clean.* Boston: Little, Brown, 2002.

Quakenbush, Robert. *Batbaby.* New York: Random House, 1997.

Ray, Mary Lyn. *Mud.* San Diego: Harcourt, 1996.

Richardson, Justin. *And Tango Makes Three.* New York: Simon and Schuster, 2005.

Roberts, Bethany. *Gramps and the Fire Dragon.* New York: Clarion, 1997.

Robertson, M. P. *The Egg.* New York: Puffin, 2000.

Rockwell, Anne. *Apples and Pumpkins.* New York: Macmillan, 1989.

_____. *Pumpkin Day, Pumpkin Night.* New York: Walker, 1999.

Rodman, Mary Ann. *My Best Friend.* New York: Viking, 2005.

Rohmann, Eric. *My Friend Rabbit.* New Milford, CT: Roaring Brook, 2002.

_____. *Pumpkinhead.* New York: Knopf, 2003.

Rose, Deborah Lee. *Ocean Babies.* Washington, DC: National Geographic, 2005.

Rosenberry, Vera. *The Growing Up Tree.* New York: Holiday House, 2003.

Ross, Tom. *Eggbert, the Slightly Cracked Egg.* New York: Putnam, 1994.

Ross, Tony. *Happy Blanket.* New York: Farrar, Straus and Giroux, 1990.

Rylant, Cynthia. *If You'll Be My Valentine.* New York: HarperCollins, 2005.

_____. *Puppy Mudge Loves His Blanket.* New York: Simon and Schuster, 2004.

Salerno, Steven. *Little Trumbo*. New York: Cavendish, 2003.

Saltzberg, Barney. *I Love Cats*. Cambridge, MA: Candlewick, 2005.

Samuels, Barbara. *Happy Valentine's Day, Dolores*. New York: Farrar, Straus and Giroux, 2006.

Sayre, April Pulley. *Crocodile Listens*. New York: Greenwillow, 2001.

Schachner, Judith Byron. *The Grannyman*. New York: Dutton, 1999.

Schaefer, Carole Lexa. *Full Moon Barnyard Dance*. Cambridge, MA: Candlewick, 2003.

Segal, John. *Carrot Soup*. New York: Margaret K. McElderry, 2006.

Serwaki. *Doorknob the Rabbit and the Carnival of Bugs*. Berkeley, CA: Tricycle Press, 2005.

Seuss, Dr. *My Many Colored Days*. New York: Knopf, 1996.

Shannon, David. *Duck on a Bike*. New York: Blue Sky Press, 2002.

Shannon, Terry Miller. *Tub Toys*. Berkeley, CA: Tricycle Press, 2002.

Sharmat, Mitchell. *Gregory the Terrible Eater*. New York: Simon and Schuster, 1980.

Shields, Carol Diggory. *The Bugliest Bug*. Cambridge, MA: Candlewick, 2002.

Shore, Diane ZuHone. *Look Both Ways: A Cautionary Tale*. New York: Bloomsbury, 2005.

Sierra, Judy. *Counting Crocodiles*. San Diego: Harcourt, 1997.

_____. *What Time Is It, Mr. Crocodile?* Orlando: Gulliver, 2004.

Silverman, Erica. *Big Pumpkin*. New York: Aladdin, 1992.

Slangerup, Erik Jon. *Dirt Boy*. Morton Grove, IL: Albert Whitman, 2000.

Sloat, Teri. *Patty's Pumpkin Patch*. New York: Putnam, 1999.

Smith, Maggie. *Paisley*. New York: Knopf, 2004.

Somers, Kevin. *Meaner Than Meanest*. New York: Hyperion, 2001.

Spinelli, Eileen. *Rise the Moon*. New York: Dial, 2003.

Spurr, Elizabeth. *Farm Life*. New York: Holiday House, 2003.

_____. *Halloween Sky Ride*. New York: Holiday House, 2005.

Squires, Janet. *The Gingerbread Cowboy*. New York: Laura Geringer, 2006.

Steig, William. *Pete's a Pizza*. New York: HarperCollins, 1998.

Stepto, Michele. *Snuggle Piggy and the Magic Blanket*. New York: Dutton, 1987.

Stevens, Janet. *The Great Fuzz Frenzy*. Orlando: Harcourt, 2005.

_____. *The Three Billy Goats Gruff*. New York: Harcourt, 1990.

Stewart, Amber. *Rabbit Ears*. New York: Bloomsbury, 2006.

Sturges, Philemon. *The Little Red Hen Makes a Pizza*. New York: Dutton, 1999.

Sweeney, Jacqueline. *Once Upon a Lily Pad*. San Francisco: Chronicle Books, 1995.

Tanis, Joel. *The Dragon Pack Snack Attack*. New York: Four Winds, 1993.

Taylor, Thomas. *The Loudest Roar*. New York: Arthur A. Levine, 2003.

Tegen, Katherine Brown. *The Story of the Easter Bunny*. New York: HarperCollins, 2005.

Thaler, Mike. *Moonkey*. New York: Harper and Row, 1981.

Thayer, Jane. *The Popcorn Dragon*. New York: Morrow, 1989.

Thomas, Eliza. *The Red Blanket*. New York: Scholastic, 2004.

Thomas, Shelley Moore. *Good Night, Good Knight*. (Series) New York: Dutton, 2000.

Thompson, Lauren. *Little Quack's Bedtime*. New York: Simon and Schuster, 2005.

_____. *Little Quack's New Friend*. New York: Simon and Schuster, 2006.

_____. *Mouse's First Snow*. New York: Simon and Schuster, 2005.

_____. *Mouse's First Valentine*. New York: Simon and Schuster, 2002.

Tomlinson, Jill. *The Owl Who Was Afraid of the Dark*. Cambridge, MA: Candlewick, 2001.

Ungerer, Tomi. *Rufus*. New York: HarperCollins, 1961.

Van Laan, Nancy. *Little Baby Bobby*. New York: Knopf, 1996.

_____. *Scrubba Dub*. New York: Atheneum, 2003.

Vaughan, Marcia. *Snap!* New York: Scholastic, 1996.

Velthuijs, Max. *Frog in Love*. New York: Farrar, Straus and Giroux, 1989.

Vrombaut, An. *Clarabella's Teeth*. New York: Clarion, 2003.

Waddell, Martin. *It's Quacking Time*. Cambridge, MA: Candlewick, 2005.

_____. *Owl Babies*. Cambridge, MA: Candlewick, 1992.

_____. *What Use Is a Moose?* Cambridge, MA: Candlewick, 1996.

Wakefield, Pat. *A Moose for Jessica*. New York: Dutton, 1987.

Wallace, Nancy Elizabeth. *Apples, Apples, Apples*. Delray Beach, FL: Winslow, 2000.

_____. *Pumpkin Day!* New York: Marshall Cavendish, 2002.

_____. *The Sun, the Moon, and the Stars*. Boston: Houghton Mifflin, 2003.

_____. *The Valentine Express*. Tarrytown, NY: Marshall Cavendish, 2004.

Walsh, Ellen Stoll. *Dot and Jabber and the Big Bug Mystery*. Orlando: Harcourt, 2003.

_____. *Mouse Paint*. San Diego: Harcourt, 1989.

Walsh, Melanie. *Do Monkeys Tweet?* Boston: Houghton Mifflin, 1997.

Walter, Virginia. *Hi, Pizza Man!* New York: Orchard, 1995.

Walton, Rick. *Mrs. McMurphy's Pumpkin.* New York: HarperFestival, 2004.

Weeks, Sarah. *Be Mine, Be Mine, Sweet Valentine.* New York: Laura Geringer, 2006.

Wellington, Monica. *Apple Farmer Annie.* New York: Dutton, 2001.

West, Colin. *Have You Seen the Crocodile?* New York: Lippincott, 1986.

_____. *Moose and Mouse.* Boston: Kingfisher, 2004.

Whatley, Bruce. *Wait! No Paint!* New York: HarperCollins, 2001.

Wheeler, Lisa. *Hokey Pokey: Another Prickly Love Story.* New York: Little, Brown, 2006.

Whiter, Barb. *Balloon Animals.* New York: Mud Puddle Books, 2003.

Wiesmuller, Dieter. *The Adventures of Marco and Polo.* New York: Walker, 2000.

Wilson, Karma. *Bear's New Friend.* New York: Margaret K. McElderry, 2006.

_____. *The Frog in the Bog.* New York: Margaret K. McElderry, 2003.

_____. *Hilda Must Be Dancing.* New York: Margaret K. McElderry, 2004.

_____. *Moose Tracks.* New York: Margaret K. McElderry, 2006.

Wolcott, Patty. *The Marvelous Mud Washing Machine.* New York: Random House, 1991.

Woloson, Eliza. *My Friend Isabelle.* Bethesda, MD: Woodbine, 2003.

Wood, A. J. *The Little Penguin.* New York: Dutton, 2001.

Wood, Audrey. *King Bidgood's in the Bathtub.* New York: Harcourt, 1985.

Yolen, Jane. *Owl Moon.* New York: Philomel, 1987.

Yorinks, Arthur. *Quack!* New York: Abrams, 2003.

Young, Amy. *Belinda the Ballerina.* New York: Viking, 2002.

Ziefert, Harriet. *Beach Party.* Maplewood, NJ: Blue Apple, 2005.

_____. *This Little Egg Went to Market.* New York: Puffin, 2003.

DISCOGRAPHY

"A-Goong Went the Little Green Frog." *Sing-A-Longs for Kids.* New York: Time-Life Music, 2000.

"All You Need Is Love." *All You Need Is Love.* Redway, CA: Music for Little People; distributed by Kid Rhino, 1999.

"The Animal Fair." *Silly Favorites.* Redway, CA: Music for Little People; distributed by Kid Rhino, 1998.

"Ants Go Marching." *Wee Sing Animals, Animals, Animals.* New York: Price Stern Sloan, 1999.

"Apples and Bananas." *One Light One Sun.* Raffi. Hollywood, CA: Shoreline/A&M, 1985.

"Baby Beluga." *Raffi on Broadway.* Raffi. Universal City, CA: Shoreline/MCA, 1993.

"Baby Bumblebee." *Wee Sing Animals, Animals, Animals.* Beall, Pamela. New York: Price Stern Sloan, 1999.

"Balloon-alloon-alloon." *I've Got a Yo-Yo.* Paxton, Tom. Cambridge, MA: Rounder Records, 1997.

"Bathtime." *Everything Grows.* Raffi. Willowdale, Ontario: Troubadour Records; distributed by A&M, 1987.

"The Bats Go Flying." *Kid's Favorite Songs 2.* New York: Sony Wonder, 2001.

"Be Kind to Your Web-Footed Friends." *Silly Favorites.* Redway, CA: Music for Little People; distributed by Kid Rhino, 1998.

"Bill Grogan's Goat." *Disney Silly Songs.* Burbank, CA: Walt Disney Records, Buena Vista Pictures Distribution, 1988.

"Bluebird." *Bottle of Sunshine.* Milkshake. Baltimore, MD: Milkshake Music, 2004.

"Blue-ey the Blue, Blue Blanket." *Pat the Bunny: Sing with Me.* New York: Sony Wonder, 1999.

"Bubble on My Snuffle." *Splish Splash.* New York: Sony Wonder, 1995.

"The Bunny Hop." *All-Time Favorite Dances.* Long Branch, NJ: Kimbo Educational, 1995.

"Carving Pumpkins." *Wee Sing for Halloween.* New York: Price Stern Sloan, 2002.

"Crocodile Rock." *Kids Rock Too.* Mr. Al. Wellington, FL: Cradle Rock, 2002.

"Dad Caught Stars." *Not Naptime.* Roberts, Justin. Chicago: Hear Diagonally, 2002.

"De Colores." *One Light One Sun.* Raffi. Hollywood, CA: Shoreline/A&M, 1985.

"Doin' the Moose." *If You Give a Moose a Muffin* (book and cassette). Numeroff, Laura Joffe. New York: HarperCollins, 1997.

"Don't Wash My Blanket." *Peek-A-Boo and Other Songs for Young Children.* Palmer, Hap. Topanga, CA: Hap-Pal Music, 1990.

"Down by the Bay." *Country Goes Raffi.* Cambridge, MA: Rounder Records, 2001.

"The Duck and the Kangaroo." *Wee Sing Animals, Animals, Animals.* New York: Price Stern Sloan, 1999.

"Eggbert, the Easter Egg." *Happy Easter Songs.* New York: Sony Music Special Products, 1996.

"Eggs." *Wee Sing Dinosaurs.* Los Angeles: Price Stern Sloan, 2002.

"Elephant Is Sitting in My Bathtub." *I Love My Shoes.* Ode, Eric. Sumner, WA: Deep Rooted Music, 2005.

"Five Green Apples." *Mainly Mother Goose.* Sharon, Lois, and Bram. Toronto: Elephant Records; Los Angeles: Drive Entertainment, 1994.

"Five Little Monkeys." *Six Little Ducks.* Long Branch, NJ: Kimbo Educational, 1997.

"Five Little Pumpkins." *Spooky Favorites.* Redway, CA: Music for Little People; distributed by Kid Rhino, 1999.

"Five Little Speckled Frogs." *Sing-A-Longs for Kids.* New York: Time-Life Music, 2000.

"Fly Little Bats." *Wee Sing for Halloween.* New York: Price Stern Sloan, 2002.

"Frère Jacques." *Toddler Tunes.* Franklin, TN: Cedarmont Kids, 2004.

"Friends Are Everywhere." *Monkey's Uncle.* Uncle Brothers. Orangeburg, NY: Blackwater Records, 2005.

"Frog Went A-Courtin'." *Sing-A-Longs for Kids.* Volume 1. New York: Time-Life Music, 2000.

"The Funny Little Bunny (with the Powder Puff Tail)." *Happy Easter Songs.* New York: Sony Music Special Products, 1996.

"The Gingerbread House." *Down the Holiday Trail.* Brewer, Teresa. Tampa, FL: MCA Special Products, 1993.

"The Gingerbread Man." *Bahamas Pajamas*. Scruggs, Joe. Austin, TX: Shadow Play, 1990.

"Gingerbread Man." *"C" Is for Cookie: Cookie's Favorite Songs*. Sesame Street. New York: Sony Wonder, 1995.

"The Goat." *Burl Ives Sings Little White Duck and Other Children's Favorites*. New York: Columbia, 1974.

"Grasshopper." *Wee Sing Animals, Animals, Animals*. New York: Price Stern Sloan, 1999.

"Grey Squirrel." *Baby-O!* Sunseri, Mary Lee. Pacific Grove, CA: Piper Grove Music, 2005.

"Here We Go Looby Loo." *50 Bestest Kids Songs*. Kenilworth, NJ: Turn Up the Music, 2002.

"Hokey Pokey." *Great Big Hits!* Sharon, Lois, and Bram. Kenilworth, NJ: Turn Up the Music, 2004.

"I Am a Pizza." *Party in the Park*. North Reading, MA: Hats Off Records, 1993.

"I Like Dirt." *Noisy Songs for Noisy Kids*. Thunderlords. Pennsauken, NJ: Disc Makers, 2005.

"I See the Moon." *Baby's Bedtime*. Collins, Judy. New York: Lightyear Records, 1990.

"I'm a Little Teapot." *50 Bestest Kids Songs*. Kenilworth, NJ: Turn Up the Music, 2002.

"I'm Proud to Be a Moose." *American Children*. Waterbury, VT: Alacazar Productions, 1989.

"Jack-o-Lantern." *Spooky Favorites*. Redway, CA: Music for Little People; distributed by Kid Rhino, 1999.

"Kicking Kangaroo." *A to Z: The Animals and Me*. Long Branch, NJ: Kimbo Educational, 1994.

"Ladybug." *Wee Sing Animals, Animals, Animals*. New York: Price Stern Sloan, 1999.

"Last Night the Moon Was Full." *Not Naptime*. Roberts, Justin. Chicago: Hear Diagonally, 2002.

"Let's Play in the Snow." *Sing a Song of Seasons*. Buchman, Rachel. Cambridge, MA: Rounder Records, 1997.

"The Lion Sleeps Tonight." *Rhythm of the Pridelands: Music Inspired by the Lion King*. Burbank, CA: Walt Disney Records, 1995.

"Little Squirrel Came Home." *The Library Boogie*. Knight, Tom. Wilseyville, NY: Tom Knight Productions; distributed by Orchard Kids, 2001.

"The Mitten Song." *Sing a Song of Seasons*. Buchman, Rachel. Cambridge, MA: Rounder Records, 1997.

Moose Tunes for Kids. Holmes, Brent. Tallahassee, FL: Father and Son Publishing, 2000.

"The More We Get Together." *Time to Sing!* Pittsburgh, PA: Center for Creative Play, 2004.

"My Chocolate Rabbit." *Happy Easter Songs*. New York: Sony Music Special Products, 1996.

"My Security Blanket." *Andy's Funky ABC's*. Morse, Andy. Glenmont, NY: Andy Morse, 2003.

"Mystery of the White Things." *Sing a Song of Seasons*. Buchman, Rachel. Cambridge, MA: Rounder Records, 1997.

"Neat Nanny Goat." *A to Z: The Animals and Me*. Gallina, Michael. Long Branch, NJ: Kimbo Educational, 1994.

"Never Smile at a Crocodile." *Six Little Ducks*. Long Branch, NJ: Kimbo Educational, 1997.

"Octopus's Garden." *All You Need Is Love*. Redway, CA: Music for Little People; distributed by Kid Rhino, 1999.

"On a Cold and Frosty Morning." *Sing a Song of Seasons*. Buchman, Rachel. Cambridge, MA: Rounder Records, 1997.

"One Elephant." *Great Big Hits!* Sharon, Lois, and Bram. Kenilworth, NJ: Turn Up the Music, 2004.

"One Little Owl." *Wee Sing Animals, Animals, Animals*. New York: Price Stern Sloan, 1999.

"The Owl and the Pussy Cat." *100 Toddler Favorites*. Burbank, CA: Music for Little People, 2005.

"Owl Lullaby." *Sing A to Z*. Sharon, Lois, and Bram. Santa Monica, CA: Drive Entertainment; Toronto: Elephant Records, 1994.

"Peanut Butter and Jelly." *Great Big Hits!* Sharon, Lois, and Bram. Kenilworth, NJ: Turn Up the Music, 2004.

"The Penguin Polka." *Dance and Sing: The Best of Nick Jr*. Los Angeles: Rhino, 2001.

"Penguins." *Fingerplays and Footplays*. Hallum, Rosemary. Freeport, NY: Educational Activities, 2001.

"Pepperoni Pizza." *Dr. Jean Sings Silly Songs*. Tampa, FL: Progressive Music Studios, 1999.

"Perfect Piggies." *Rhinoceros Tap: Seriously Silly Songs*. New York: Workman, 2004.

"Peter Cottontail." *Happy Easter Songs*. New York: Sony Music Special Products, 1996.

"Pizza Pie Song." *Disney Silly Songs*. Burbank, CA: Walt Disney Records; Buena Vista Pictures Distribution, 1988.

"Pizza Pizzazz." *Pizza Pizzazz*. Allard, Peter and Ellen. Worcester, MA: Walnut Hill Studio, 2006.

"Puff the Magic Dragon." *Peter, Paul, and Mommy*. Peter, Paul, and Mary. Burbank, CA: Warner Bros., 1990.

"Pumpkin, Pumpkin." *Wee Sing for Halloween*. New York: Price Stern Sloan, 2002.

"Rhinoceros Tap." *Rhinoceros Tap: Seriously Silly Songs*. Boynton, Sandra. New York: Workman, 2004.

"A Rock Hopper Penguin." *Come Dance by the Ocean*. Jenkins, Ella. Washington, DC: Smithsonian/Folkways; Cambridge, MA: Rounder Records, 1992.

"Rubber Duckie." *Splish Splash*. New York: Sony Wonder, 1995.

"Sally and the Dragon." *The Library Boogie*. Knight, Tom. Wilseyville, NY: Tom Knight Productions; distributed by Orchard Kids, 2001.

"Shake My Sillies Out." *More Singable Songs*. Raffi. Universal City, CA: Shoreline/MCA, 1977.

"The Silly Dance Contest." *Jim Gill Sings the Sneezing Song and Other Contagious Tunes.* Oak Park, IL: Gill Music, 1993.

"Six Little Ducks." *Animal Songs.* St. Laurent, Quebec: Madacy, 2004.

"Snapping Turtle." *Silly Favorites.* Redway, CA: Music for Little People; distributed by Kid Rhino, 1998.

"Song About Slow, Song About Fast." *Walter the Waltzing Worm.* Palmer, Hap. Freeport, NY: Activity Records, 1991.

"Stars." *Baby's Bedtime.* Collins, Judy. New York: Lightyear Records, 1990.

"Swing, Shake, Twist, and Stretch." *Walter the Waltzing Worm.* Palmer, Hap. Freeport, NY: Activity Records, 1991.

"Ten in the Bed." *Great Big Hits!* Sharon, Lois, and Bram. Kenilworth, NJ: Turn Up the Music, 2004.

"Ten Little Indians." *40 Kindergarten Playtime Hits.* La Crosse, WI: Platinum Disc, 2003.

"There's a Hippo in My Tub." *Bathtime Magic.* Bartels, Joanie. Van Nuys, CA: Discovery Music, 1989.

"Three Little Fishes." *Bathtime Magic.* Bartels, Joanie. Van Nuys, CA: Discovery Music, 1989.

"Three Little Kittens." *Animal Songs.* St. Laurent, Quebec: Madacy, 2004.

"The Three Little Pigs Blues." *Playing Favorites.* Greg and Steve. Cypress, CA: Youngheart Records, 1991.

"A Thump, a Twinkle, and a Twitch, or, How to Make a Rabbit." *Happy Easter Songs.* New York: Sony Music Special Products, 1996.

"Tie Me Kangaroo Down Sport." *Wiggly, Wiggly World.* The Wiggles. New York: Koch Entertainment, 2003.

"Turkey Love Song." *Rhinoceros Tap: Seriously Silly Songs.* Boynton, Sandra. New York: Workman, 2004.

"Twinkle, Twinkle, Little Star." *Baby's Bedtime.* Collins, Judy. New York: Lightyear Records, 1990.

"Under the Sea." *The Little Mermaid.* Burbank, CA: Walt Disney Records, 1989.

"Walk Like an Elephant." *Songs from JoJo's Circus.* Burbank, CA: Walt Disney Records, 2004.

"Waltz of the Flowers." *The Classical Child at the Ballet.* Mill Valley, CA: Sophia Sounds, 1997.

"We're Going to Be Friends." *Curious George and Friends: Sing-a-longs and Lullabies.* New York: Universal Records, 2005.

"Wheels on the Bus." *Toddler Tunes: 25 Classic Songs for Toddlers.* Franklin, TN: Cedarmont Kids, 2004.

"Where Do They Make Balloons." *No!* They Might Be Giants. Cambridge, MA: Rounder Records, 2002.

"Who's Afraid of the Big Bad Wolf?" *Classic Disney.* Burbank, CA: Walt Disney Records, 1999.

"Why Can't Dirt Just Leave Me Alone?" *More Songs from Jim Henson's Bear in the Big Blue House.* Burbank, CA: Walt Disney Records, 2002.

"The World We Love." *Bananaphone.* Raffi. Universal City, CA: Shoreline/MCA, 1994.

"You Are My Sunshine." *Wiggle Worms Love You.* Chicago: Old Town School Recordings, 2005.

"You Can Never Go Down the Drain." *Bathtime Magic.* Bartels, Joanie. Van Nuys, CA: Discovery Music, 1989.

INDEX

Diane Briggs has worked in public and school libraries for eighteen years and is now the owner of an online business located at http://www.librarygames.net. She has created two library game CDs entitled *I Love Books* and *Library Lollapalooza* for elementary school children and their librarians. A graduate of the School of Information Science at the State University of New York at Albany, Briggs is also the author of four other books: *101 Fingerplays, Stories, and Songs to Use with Finger Puppets* and *52 Programs for Preschoolers* were published by ALA Editions; *Toddler Storytime Programs* and *Flannelboard Fun* were published by Scarecrow Press.

Thomas Briggs is a freshman at Hudson Valley Community College in Troy, New York. He is studying fine arts.